Sail and Motor Boats:
Easy Solutions to
Onboard Problems

Hans Mühlbauer

Sail and Motor Boats: Easy Solutions to Onboard Problems

4880 Lower Valley Road • Atglen, PA 19310

Other Schiffer Books on Related Subjects:

Advanced First Aid Afloat, 5th Edition, 978-08703-3524-2, $16.99

Diesel Engines: An Owner's Guide to Operations and Maintenance,
978-0-7643-3705-5, $19.99

Segel- und Motorboote Bordprobleme einfach gelöst, written by Hans Mühlbauer, was originally published by Pietsch Verlag. This edition was translated into English by Omicron Language Solutions LLC.

Picture credits: All photos by Gerlinde Neuhierl and Hans Mühlbauer

Library of Congress Control Number: 2013937939

Type set in Univers/Serifa BT

ISBN: 978-0-7643-4425-1
Printed in China

Published by Schiffer Publishing, Ltd.
4880 Lower Valley Road
Atglen, PA 19310
Phone: (610) 593-1777; Fax: (610) 593-2002
E-mail: Info@schifferbooks.com

For our complete selection of fine books on this and related subjects, please visit our website at www.schifferbooks.com. You may also write for a free catalog.

This book may be purchased from the publisher. Please try your bookstore first.

We are always looking for people to write books on new and related subjects. If you have an idea for a book, please contact us at proposals@schifferbooks.com

Schiffer Publishing's titles are available at special discounts for bulk purchases for sales promotions or premiums. Special editions, including personalized covers, corporate imprints, and excerpts can be created in large quantities for special needs. For more information, contact the publisher.

In Europe, Schiffer books are distributed by
Bushwood Books
6 Marksbury Ave.
Kew Gardens
Surrey TW9 4JF England
Phone: 44 (0) 20 8392 8585; Fax: 44 (0) 20 8392 9876
E-mail: info@bushwoodbooks.co.uk
Website: www.bushwoodbooks.co.uk

Contents

Preface

Sailing and boating are not reinvented every time a new book comes onto the market. But new technologies and materials open up new and undreamed of possibilities on board a yacht. Traditional methods can be replaced by a simple modern component—new technology can simplify once cumbersome tasks. But there are also clever or unusual ways to use everyday items to solve problems, which at first seemed difficult.

When buying or chartering yachts, people are often focused on the dazzling looks of the vessel and on the price, not on solving complicated problems once on board. But solutions reguiring an expert can be costly, therefore many times skippers and crew themselves are often asked to find creative solutions for individual onboard problems.

Those who keep their eyes open and look around a boat in a critical way will quickly see a whole range of items in need of improvement. Using a little ingenuity, and sometimes some handicraft, many onboard issues can be simplified and made safer.

And thus, throughout my many sailing years, I have collected my own little guide for onboard practice, which, together with ideas gathered on other yachts, I have combined in this volume. I would like to thank my partner Gerlinde Neuhierl for her photography, her forbearance while I was busy writing, and above all her active cooperation in the editorial work.

I hope you find this book practical and enjoy adapting the 212 tips included here for your own onboard problems. If you have developed your own solution for any onboard issues, write to me about it. For comments or questions, contact me at hans.muehlbauer@dmcreisen.de or 49-0821-711124.

–Hans Mühlbauer

1. Light and Shade

Retractable Sun Awning

In the warm season, sun protection is essential when on board. Nowadays stable bimini tops, which stay in place while sailing, offer shade on many yachts.
Cruising sailors who spend long periods at anchor or in the marina, may also rig a sun awning over the saloon to keep the area below deck as cool as possible. These days the majority of mainsails have lazy jacks, which prevent a large sail panel from being laid over the main-boom and firmly lashed to the stanchions as was previously done.

Tip
Resourceful people have two smaller sun awnings customized, which are attached, respectively, to both sides of the main-boom and spanned sideways towards the railing. In order to simplify the daily setup and breakdown, this sun awning is simply rolled-up to the boom and stored in a tube with a zip. Those who don't like zips, can achieve the same result using short bungee cords.

A Sun Awning Made from a Dinghy Sail

We Central-Europeans do love the Southern sun a lot. After the long, cold winter days, we long for light. However, too much sunlight is not healthy, and we quickly find it too hot. Here a sun awning

The roll-up awning even provides protection in the rain.

A jib serves as sun shade (above and below).

or bimini top on board a yacht is ideal. In addition, the retractable sun awning also provides protection from rain. However, the bimini top obstructs the view of the sail above and thus makes steering difficult. And a sun awning can only be set up when the mainsail is not set.

Tip

For this situation, I carry an old dinghy jib on board that functions as a small sun

shade that can be set up anywhere. I have tied a 6.5' (2 m) lanyard to each of the three corners of the sail. I can thus instantly set this sun shade nearly anywhere on board: at the helm, over the cockpit, over the bow, or as shade for the saloon window. The best part is that I can roll up the cloth into a very small roll and it takes up very little space in the aft-locker.

A Lanyard for Your Cap

For many watersports enthusiasts, a good sun hat is indispensable, it is one of the first lines of defense for effective protection from the burning rays of the sun. Particularly popular is the baseball cap, since these are available quite cheaply nearly everywhere and the large bill offers good face protection. But the ears remain unprotected and thus many a sailor has at least once received a set of "hot ears" after a sunny day of sailing. These caps have another disadvantage: A gust of wind can quickly "reach" under the brim and rip the lift the hat overboard.

Tip

To avoid being left unprotected upon losing a cap, keep a reserve cap on hand or attach a safety lanyard to the cap, preventing it from being lost. A 1.5' (40–50 cm) piece of whipping twine can be used as an effective lanyard. Fuse the ends of the twine with a lighter to prevent fraying and sew it directly to the cap.

You can also create a version where the lanyard is merely clipped on. Use a small clip from the hardware store for this. Normally one uses these clips to attach to towels in order to provide the towels

With a lanyard in place, your head cover won't fly away.

A Lanyard for Your Glasses

As a snorkeling-experienced skipper I once had to go looking for a pair of expensive glasses in the harbor of Kos, which one of my co-sailors lost while looking in the water. Full of enthusiasm for the task at hand, I jumped into the brown stew and luckily found the valuable item immediately. I have since avoided such search and recovery missions.

Tip

At the start of a trip, co-sailors who wear glasses, including sun glasses, receive a piece of whipping twine with an urgent request to attach the 1.5' (0.5 m) piece of twine to their glasses.

In this way important items remain on each person and I am spared excursions to exotic diving locations.

This action of tying on a lanyard also incorporates nicely into the section "applied knots" because a knot is not just a knot: Either the knot slips and the glasses catcher is useless or it puts unwanted pressure on the temple. After

with a loop for hanging. Once clipped to the cap, simply tie the whipping twine to the clip.

Those who attend conferences and trade shows are surely familiar with name badges that clip to a jacket. If you cut away the name badge and attach the safety lanyard instead, you end up with a good connection between your cap and the lanyard.

There are other ways of attaching the safety lanyard. Attach the lanyard to the left and right sides of the cap so the resulting loop is worn behind the neck. This version is not entirely effective: If you look up at the mast the wind could blow the cap off backwards, never to be seen again. In another version one end of the safety lanyard is attached to the back of the cap while the other is clipped to the collar or elsewhere on the clothing. Now the cap can fly off one's head, but it remains hanging on the lanyard and thus is easily retrieved. (A shame actually, because with such a well secured cap, the crew never gets to enjoy a spontaneous "cap-over-board maneuver.")

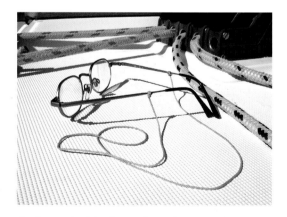

A piece of whipping twine will do the job.

a few attempts, it has become clear that a fisherman's bend does the trick. Tied tightly to the thinnest part of the temples, this knot doesn't slip, doesn't loosen accidentally nor does it press uncomfortably against your head.

Baseball Cap under the Hood

Bad weather is not everyone's cup of tea and even diehards become cranky when they're soaked to the skin. Great foul-weather clothing for the entire body is available, only the face has to remain open, and at the same time this is the problem. When you have pulled the hood of the oilskins over, it is true that the back of your head and your ears are well protected, but you cannot really hear what the skipper is saying and your whole face still receives every drop of water.

Tip

Just by putting on a simple baseball cap before pulling over the hood, the face is effectively protected from rain and sea spray. If the cap is made of a cloth material, after a while it will soak up water beneath the hood and dampen your hair. In this event I replace the cap with a second baseball cap I keep on hand.

Glare-Free Cockpit Lighting

After a good day of sailing, the crew will often happily sit in the cockpit on a warm summer evening to relax. To light this space you may use lamps that hang or lamps that

The baseball cap under the hood is not a very fashionable look, but it's extremely practical.

sit on the table, and which can be fueled by electricity, petroleum, or wax.

It is, however, unfortunate that all of these lighting devices have to be carried as extra equipment and set up and dismantled, and that they can be rather bright and thus have a slight blinding effect on the crew.

Tip

The camper accessories market offers an affordable and non-blinding solution: namely license plate lights! These small lights are

License plate lights for campers are useful on board and don't give off too much glare.

provided with a 10-watt globe. This is even enough light for reading and perfect for creating a cheerful mood in an intimate circle. The housing is made of stainless steel for withstanding salted roads, thus also making it sturdy for salty sea air and water. The rest is made of plastic and they usually cost under $10 a piece.

As required, you can choose to mount one or more of these license plate lights in appropriate locations in the cockpit with the light shining down. The indirect light illuminates the area without shining directly into the eyes.

Below deck and even when night sailing, these anti-glare lights have proven to be the best.

Drink koozie

Drink Koozies

If you have stowed away canned beverages for the trip, you may be familiar with the problem of drinks quickly becoming warm after removing them from the refrigerator or cooler. Cans can also slide around with light pounding or rolling of the boat and/or fall over, usually creating a mess.

Tip

In Australia, if you ask for a drink koozie, you may be rewarded with a bottle of beer over the counter.

And since "down under" it is mostly hot, you drink the beer straight from the bottle, but you still receive a koozie. This is an insulated container for bottles or cans that is typically made from Styrofoam or neoprene, the same material that wet-suits are made of. A rubber koozie is a practical aid on board: The drink is well insulated and thus stays cold, and because of the rubber it doesn't slide around as easily on the bare table.

Solar Panels on the Roof

Electricity from solar energy is a wonderful thing. The solar cells fill the batteries in an eco-friendly and silent way. They are, however, very expensive to buy and take up a lot of space on board, and in particular, the places where sun worshippers love to sunbathe.

Tip

On permanently inhabited cruising yachts that spend long periods on a mooring, an appropriately sized solar panel on deck provides an ideal energy source.

But for yachts which are either moved daily or lie unused on the dock during the week, a small solar setup is fully sufficient.

If the yacht is sailed daily with the motor in use, then the electric supply from the alternator, which charges the battery, should be enough. In the case of yachts that are not used much, a small solar panel is enough to slowly charge the battery during the week so that fully charged batteries will be ready for the weekend.

Only a suitably sized solar panel can keep the freezer running.

when the heated air cools down and the moisture contained therein precipitates in the form of evening clouds. This moisture accumulates on board in the form of dew on the deck. If the ceiling hatches are not closed in time, then the bunks below them will also receive their share of condensation.

Tip
It is especially important to shut the ceiling hatches before going out for dinner. Thus the mattresses and blankets will stay nice and dry.

In most cases a small solar setup with a 10- or 20-watt capacity will be enough to not only guarantee the supply of a trickle charge to the batteries, but also to give an additional charge to the onboard power storage. The fact that such a small setup can be acquired inexpensively also suits the owner's wallet.

Hatches Shut During Twilight

In the evening, back on board after a visit to the cozy local pub, there is nothing better than to snuggle up in the comfortable bunk and gently drift off to sleep. It is not so comfortable however, when the evening dew has crept into the fabric and unpleasantly dampened the bedding. This happens in the evening

Dampness creeps into the yacht through open hatches.

Without sun-protection it can get really sweaty.

Shade in the Late Afternoon

Especially in the warm and tropical sailing regions, such as the Mediterranean, the Caribbean, the Seychelles, and around Australia, effective sun protection is a must. On many yachts you will find a bimini top, which does protect the cockpit from the burning midday sun, but also spoils the helmsman's view of the sail above. The later it is in the afternoon, the closer the sun lies to the horizon—the sun's rays are less inclined, making the bimini useless.

Tip
Various auxiliary structures can be put to use here.
Bedsheets, large towels, or a sarong can be used as a sun shade. There are several ways to attach the shade to shrouds and stays:

▶ The simplest way is to pin the corners of the cloth to the steel cables with clothes pins. However, this structure can slip down quickly because of a lack of grip, and with the slightest puff of wind...the beautiful cloth will fly away. Thus this is only a solution for the doldrums.

▶ If using a relatively thin material, attach the sun shade to the back stay with a half-hitch which is tied with the cloth itself. Although this holds pretty well, it does tend to slide down.

▶ Those who tie the makeshift sun shade to the shrouds and stays using bungee cords will be popular because this holds up very well, even in wind—sometimes so well that the cloth may start to rip under the wind's force.

Incidentally: The tender, if set up on the foredeck using the spinnaker halyard, shades the foredeck hatch, acts as a wind shelter, funnels fresh air below deck, and in rainy weather serves as a rain shelter so the hatch underneath it can be opened for ventilation.

Shade on Board

For many, boating is above all a summer activity, since the real pleasure in sailing and motor-boating only truly comes with sun and pleasant temperatures. In the height of summer, and in the southern regions, the burning sun can, however, quickly become a problem. Shade has to be provided.

Tip

Besides the sun awnings or bimini tops that are usually found on yachts, a simple beach umbrella can also provide pleasant shade. Such an umbrella can be found in any tourist shop on the beach for cheap. The metal

A beach umbrella may look funny on board, but it does serve its purpose.

parts may rust in time, but for a few years you will enjoy the shade your umbrella provides.

The beach umbrella can be mounted in many ways: It can easily be sail-tied to the stanchions wherever it may be needed at the time. In the cockpit, for example, you can lash it to the steering pedestal, in order to protect the helmsman from the sun on longer trips.

The shaft of the umbrella can be attached semi-permanently using pipe clamps and the actual umbrella, which is stored in the aft locker, can simply be slipped in.

Sun Protection in the Saloon

When sailing in southern regions, the body longs for coolness and shade. In the summer it can become fairly hot and stuffy directly below deck.

Tip

Cheap roller shades sold in auto part stores provide invaluable shade for window surfaces and deck-hatches. They are attached on the inside, most with just two screws. Use a third screw to hold the shade open. Inside the shade there is a spring which keeps the fabric taut when open. This works for both vertical or horizontal mounting. When not in use, the material simply rolls back into the roll and is hardly noticeable.

The material is permeable, so that air continues to circulate even when the shade is being used.

If after a few years of sea air the spring mechanism of the shade becomes rusted, you can purchase a replacement at the nearest service station or auto parts store. There are also special aluminized roller shades that reflect the sun's heat even more effec-

Without sun protection the saloon can become really stuffy.

the flames, these rolls catch oil splashes. Here they can also be rolled away when not in use. And when the material becomes unsightly, just cut off a piece of the roll and re-thread the rest, because these rolls are sold in lengths starting at about 5.5' (1.7 m), which is far too long for onboard use. But when cut off they can provide many years of use.

tively. But these devices are significantly more expensive and are neither light nor air permeable, preventing fresh air from entering the yacht interior. But these aluminized shades can be put to use elsewhere on your vessel: as a splash guard above and around the stove. Mounted out of range of

It Stays Dry under the Sun Awning

Tip

A sun awning or a permanently installed bimini top is part of the standard equipment on yachts in warmer regions. The sun shade is quickly setup at the anchorage or in the marina and provides cooling shade.

A bimini can even remain set up when sail-

ing, provided it doesn't interfere with the boom. And these useful devices also offer protection in case of a downpour, helping ensure that the cockpit remains relatively dry. But not only this: In the early evening, before the dew starts to form in the cockpit, the Bimini foils the dew's plans of forming on the cockpit seats. And so the guests and crew can enjoy their sundowners on board without getting a wet behind.

The crew can work under a sun shade or sit and relax until late at night without getting wet.

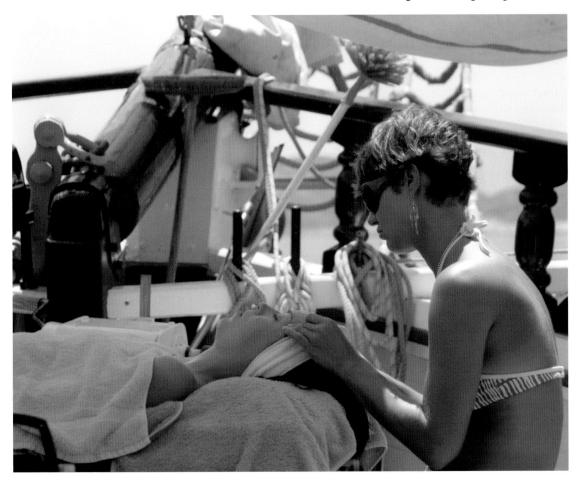

Relaxing massage under a sun shade.

2. Sail and Rigging

...And There Goes the Mast

It can happen quickly, unexpectedly the mast comes down. Not in heavy weather, but as the sails are being taken in, as the yacht is sailing towards the anchorage in the lee of a Greek island. The skipper—sailing single-handed—starts the engine while the autopilot keeps the yacht straight into the wind and he then starts to furl away the foresail with the roller furler. Then it happens: The furler snags a little, the skipper pulls at the furling line with force, there is a snap, and the mast tilts a little backwards, the forestay has said goodbye. Now only the foresail is holding up the mast. The skipper runs forward to support the mast with the spinnaker halyard, but too late! Slowly, because the mainsail acts as a parachute,

the entire rig collapses towards the stern and then crashes down on the stern railing. Luckily nothing else happened, but what was the reason for the forestay giving way?

Tip

The furling jib is used daily. Around the cable forestay there is an aluminum section around which the sailcloth is wound. This section is assembled using stainless-steel bolts. These bolts reach into the forestay cable and with each turn the forestay is twisted by this torsion. Most often the forestay cable snaps immediately above or below the cable terminal. In any case, the forestay can only be inspected if one takes down and completely disassembles the roller furling system, but who does that? And so, unknown to the skipper, the individual wires of the forestay cable can systematically break until the unit is too weak and finally snaps. The mast then falls over.

Regular rig-inspection helps to avoid this situation.

Since inspecting the forestay is only possible with much effort, one has to focus on
other signs that deterioration has begun.
When the first wires have been severed,
the furler will only turn with difficulty—it
catches on the wires. It is then high time
for a check! Because otherwise it is either
the plastic drum or the bearings which are
kaput.

DIY Barber Hauler

On many courses of sail one wishes for better control and trim possibilities for the foresail, the gennaker, or spinnaker. But not all
yachts, especially not charter yachts, offer
the availability of regatta-standard trimming tools.

Tip

A barber hauler provides a simply made, but
effective, trimming tool. It provides additional control of the sheeting point of the
sail, allowing it to be adjusted further out-
or inboard or further forward or aft.
There are various possibilities for setting up
this trim line.

▶ Attached to the toe rail for example. Many
of these aluminum fixtures already have
appropriate perforation, which simplifies
the attachment of the barber hauler. Of
course one can also drill a hole at the
appropriate location in a non-perforated
toe rail.
▶ There are also stable deck fittings on
the coach roof of many yachts which are
meant as a base point for the barber hauler. Of course on your own yacht you can
mount a deck fitting at almost any point
your heart desires.
▶ The chain plates could also be considered
for this purpose.

Either a sail tie, a shackle, or a carabiner
is attached to this base point. The best
method, however, is the use of a block,
which reduces friction when paying-out
and sheeting-in the trimline. When it has
to happen fast, or when there is no block
available, then the barber hauler can also
be led straight through the shackle or carabiner. The one end of the trimming line can
either be attached directly to the clew of the
genoa, jib, spinnaker, or gennaker, or it is
left to run freely on the sheet using a further
(snatch-) block. The other end is led back to
the cockpit where it can either be led onto a
winch or a cleat. The barber hauler, as effective trimming tool, is also useful to charterers seeing as except for a shackle and a few
meters of relatively thin line, no additional
technology is needed for the basic version
and it only takes a few minutes to set up.

Two blocks, a piece of line, and the setup is complete.

A Block for All Occasions

Many times a line will engage exactly where there is no deck fitting available. It should be somehow diverted. For optimal trim the foresail needs a sheeting point which cannot be provided by the jib sheet track, or the spinnaker sheet needs a barber hauler to keep the massive canvas in check. But what can you do?

Tip

It's very simple! Just use:

▶ One simple block (if you want to get fancy, use a snatch block, this sometimes keeps you from threading a few lines through) and
▶ A line about 3.3' to 6.5' (1 to 2 m) long, and the mobile block for all occasions is ready. Using the line, this block should be attached to cleats, chain plates, or any other strong point on deck.

The jib or spinnaker sheet then runs through the block and just like that an effective barber hauler has been created without much effort.

Cunningham for the Jib Luff

That which has been deemed as good on many regatta yachts cannot be bad for the cruising sailor. Trim specialists adjust the foresail luff tension according to wind strength and angle. How does that work?

Tip

Use the jib halyard for this. Because of the large amounts of force needed, one has to tighten it up on a winch; however, these are typically occupied. One can also set up a short purchase system between the tack and the deck fitting. Depending on ship and sail size, this purchase is more or less adjustable towards the least required effort. Lead the here-incorporated line to the cockpit and secure it there.

A block can be lashed on almost anywhere.

A taut luff installed with little effort.

From here on out, the setting of the jib can take place without using the winch, because only the sailcloth has to be hoisted. When that happens, the luff tensioner is in any case only pulled tight by hand, until the desired luff tension has been achieved. During the sail, the tension can be adjusted using just one hand at any time.

For your information: For the tensioning of the luff tension of the mainsail, a cunningham is often used—a hook with a trim line tied to it, which is hooked to a cringle in the bottom area of the luff (specially provided for the purpose). The same applies for the foresail.

Going up the Mast

Is the crew too weak, or are you sailing solo? Every now and again it happens that the skipper—or often the lightest crew member—has to go up the mast, to clear a halyard, to inspect the shrouds, or to do maintenance on bolts and screws. And there the problems begin: Who is the lightest? Who doesn't have vertigo? Who is actually qualified to do the work at hand? And regarding the deck-crew: Do they have enough power and stamina to hoist him/her/them up?

Only sailors without vertigo should go up the mast.

Tip

In order to find the solution for this problem, let's think of an old windjammer. There were no mechanical or electrical winches. All problems of force were solved with purchase systems. According to the force needed, one or multiple-disk blocks with corresponding lengths of ropework were incorporated, together with a larger or smaller number of sailors to heave on the purchase system.

In this way even very large sail areas and loads amounting to tons could be controlled.

Even in modern times a purchase, for example on the mainsail halyard, can be hoisted to the top of the mast.

▶ The boson's chair is attached to the bottom end wherein the "mast-climber" takes his/her seat.

▶ Depending on the purchase ratio, it is now even easy for non-bodybuilders to hoist a person up. And, starting from a ratio of approx. 4:1 the mast climber can even hoist him/herself aloft.

▶ A correspondingly set-up main halyard purchase with integrated cam cleat is good for this purpose, because the boson's chair can be fixed at any desired height.

▶ One should not go without an additional safety knot in case of accidental loosening of the cleat.

▶ Just as important is a helper on deck who additionally assures the entire action with a secondary halyard which is also attached to the boson's chair.

Thus prepared and carried out, the mast action can be performed efficiently—even by small crews.

When the Topping Lift Sings

The topping lift is one of the most important "members of the crew" on board any sailing yacht.

Without the topping lift the boom would lie in the cockpit.

It is responsible for keeping the boom in position when the sail isn't set. It is also responsible for assuring that the boom swings around high over the heads of the crew.

In the daytime, when sailing, it can and should hang around loosely, but in the evening and at night in the anchorage, it should be set tight. But sometimes during these long evening hours it can get bored and when it is furthermore stroked by a light evening breeze, it softly starts to sing. And when the night-breeze truly sets in and its strength increases, this is also the signal for the topping lift to turn up the volume. But finally, the crew's night rest becomes an issue and an attempt is made to quiet down the singing topping lift.

Tip

The topping lift is known to be the line which reaches from the top of the mast to the tip of the boom and thereby holds up the weight of the boom. Depending on how tight the mainsheet is sheeted in, the topping lift will also be more or less taut. In any case, the effect is like that of a tensioned guitar string, and when the wind causes this string to vibrate, a more or less high pitched tone is produced. The pitch of the tone is dependent on the length of the string and on its tension. The yacht hull furthermore acts as the body of the guitar and amplifies the vibration, so that it can be heard very clearly, everywhere. This can be remedied by disturbing the vibration of the string, i.e. the topping lift. This can be achieved by:

▶ Lightly easing out the main-sheet, or
▶ Tying-on short pieces of line or material to the topping lift.

And so the vibration, and thus the tone, can be completely eliminated and the night's rest assured.

Doubled-Up Sheets

In a stiff breeze, the foresail trimmers struggle with the jib winch, but only with great effort is the foresail tightly set. Progress is made by the inch. Not considering the fact that the helmsman could help by heading up a touch in order to take the pressure out of the sail and leaving the trimmers to crank on almost effortlessly, the effort needed is simply too much for most. Naturally, one could install larger winches, self-tailing of course, perhaps even triple-geared, or even electrically powered, but winches are just so expensive! What to do?

Tip

For a fraction of the cost there is an alternative: Use doubled-up sheets. A simple block is attached to the clew of the foresail. First tie the jib sheet to the sheeting point, then lead through the block, and only then bring it back onto the jib-winch. With this simple setup, you have increased efficiency by a whopping 50 percent! This means that only half the power is now needed.

Here, a smaller sized winch could even be chosen.

There are additional savings when it comes to the jib sheet: this line can now be significantly thinner and thus less expensive. However, it has to be thick enough for one to get a good grip by hand. All in all, this solution provides great relief and requires little time and money. And he, who knows a clever sail maker, can have a double-block (with two big disks) built directly into the clew.

A Bucket as Yacht Stabilizer

Not every anchorage is so calm that yachts don't sway in the swell there. This back and forth movement in the swell can often rob crew of sleep or even cause their stomachs to rebel.

Tip

A remedy, or at least a marked improvement, can be achieved with the use of a simple plastic bucket. First, ease out the spinnaker pole horizontally until it is 90 degrees to the hull.

Doubled-up sheets only need half the power.

A bucket used as a stabilizer can dampen a yacht's roll.

Tie a bucket to the end of the pole with a line that is long enough to ensure that the bucket is well submerged. To ensure that it sinks and doesn't end up floating around on the surface, place a large stone inside the bucket to weigh it down. When set up in this way, the "stabilizer bucket" reduces the rolling action of the yacht very effectively.

In case this measure does not suffice, rig another bucket on the opposite side of the yacht. On large motor yachts and cruise liners, real stabilizers are used instead of buckets, but the principle is fairly similar.

A Halyard as Anchor Watchman

Should we, or shouldn't we? Many skippers ask themselves the question of the need for an anchor watch when lying at anchor in uncertain wind and weather conditions. Especially with small crews, the boring night watch doesn't really help improve fitness or moral. A simple yet proven trick helps contribute to an extensive, undisturbed nights' rest.

The halyard starts rattling when the wind picks up.

Tip

Every sailor knows the rattling of halyards in the marina. This noise is disturbing, nerve wracking, and sleep depriving. But what if one "tunes" one's own main halyard in such a way that, in calm, slight seas and moderate wind, it remains quiet and well behaved and only starts its disturbing rattling at five on the Beaufort scale? For this purpose, the halyard is set a small distance away from the mast and tightened with corresponding force. Distance and tension are to be determined through experimentation in corresponding wind strengths, because every rig behaves differently.

The result of this measure is that the skipper and crew can indulge in well-deserved sleep in calm weather. If the wind should, however, pick up and a monitoring presence becomes necessary, the main halyard starts to wake sailors up and get them on deck. Now you can decide whether or not a permanent anchor watch is necessary.

A cautious skipper would of course set his/her alarm every two hours in order to have a quick check. But thanks to the "anchor watchman halyard" he can also get his/her beauty sleep.

A Situation for the Pilot-Line

One of the biggest disasters on board is the snapping of a halyard. Not only will a sail suddenly come crashing down, but an important question immediately comes up: "How am I going to feed a new halyard through the mast?"

Tip

Whatever happens, someone will have to go up to the top of the mast. Sometimes, probably seldom, a runged mast is part of the equation, which simplifies the situation. In most cases a crew member is winched up the mast in order to feed a new halyard through. But such a thick line doesn't let itself be fed through the mast that easily. A pilot line helps.

- ▶ It consists of a length of strong whipping line, which has to be a little bit longer than the height of the mast.
- ▶ The end is weighted down, for example, with an M 8 or M 10 sized nut, or a small fishing weight.
- ▶ The person in the rig feeds this pilot line over the proper pulley in the mast and slowly lowers it down.
- ▶ At the foot of the mast, a second person fishes the line from the mast opening using a simple wire that is bent at the end.
- ▶ Now he/she can tie on the new halyard and then the person in the rig can pull it to the top.
- ▶ With regard to durability, the whipping knot has proved itself—it closely clings to the thicker halyard cord, easily pulls the halyard over the pulley in the mast, and is easy to untie afterwards.
- ▶ If you are afraid that the thin safety line won't be able to support the heavy line, then feed the new halyard from the top to the bottom.

Jib Sheets as Grab Lines

On many yachts with furling systems, when furled away, the jib sheets hang loose on

A beautiful whipping-knot.

Except for the jib sheets, there is nothing at the bow.

the deck and the ends are also often left unsecured. But lines lying loose on deck create an opportunity for accidents to happen. First, they are a tripping-hazard, and second, they roll out from beneath those who step on them so that crew members find themselves lying on deck with at least a few bruises. But the problem is easy to solve.

Tip
Jib sheets can also serve a safety purpose. For this, after the furling-away of the jib, the furling line is first pulled tight and secured, then it is the jib sheets' turn. They are also pulled moderately tight, secured, and the ends are coiled. Now nothing is left lying loose on deck. The advantage of this is that, especially when working on the unsteady bow, one can hold onto the sheets when one's own balance is at risk.

Main Boom Brace at Anchorage

When the mainsail is not set, the boom is, as a rule, prevented from falling by the topping lift and from swinging horizontally by the tightened mainsheet. Those who are lying in a "rolly" anchorage or in a harbor with lots of swell are sure to become desperate because of the sounds caused by the light swinging of the boom with each swell.

Tip
Further tightening of the mainsheet won't solve anything here. But a safety line run from the end of the boom to one of the stern-cleats provides the cure. If the mainsheet is payed out a little and the line correspondingly tightened, the boom is fixed in the resulting y-formed bridle and the swinging stops immediately.

Mainsail Set with Half the Force

Every sailor knows the effort involved in hoisting and lowering the mainsail. But practice shows that there are effective aids which can reduce the effort involved.

Tip
There are two possibilities for more efficiently handling the heavy mainsail.
On many yachts a standard furling mainsail is already installed, i.e. a mast, into which the specially designed main is furled. Handling is conceivably simple—as long as

A boom-brace prevents annoying swinging and creaking.

A turning block on the sail head makes child's play out of setting the sail.

the system works well, which fortunately it does most of the time. But sail area and cut are not as effective as with a conventional mainsail.

The performance data is certainly not comparable with a battened main. Here the sail area can turn out to be several square feet larger, and thanks to the battens, the profile performs very effectively in the wind. The disadvantage, however, is the comparably greater weight of this variation.

In order to relieve the crew of the setting of this truly heavy sail, one can simply shackle a block to the head of the sail. The main halyard runs through this and thereby forms a simple purchase system with a ratio of 1:2. This means that only half of the previously used power is needed when hoisting. The halyard needs to be double the length, however.

It is really amazing how easy the setting of the main suddenly becomes—this is also ideal for the small (family) crew.

Jammed Mainsail

The majority of charter yachts commissioned in the Mediterranean have sail furling systems. As practical as these devices might be, they can also quickly present problems, mainly at the least convenient times. The furling main is regularly furled into the mast and this into a narrow chamber into which the sail cloth has to squeeze. If the boom is not held completely horizontal by the topping lift or kicker while furling, or when the sail flaps too much, then it is inevitable that a fold in the sail will block the entire furling system, and nothing goes anymore. If the wind were to freshen, this situation could quickly become extremely dangerous.

The only thing that works here is going aloft.

Tip

Pulling hard on the control-lines will not help.

▶ Many try to force the sail in or out using a winch, but this only aggravates the problem and can lead to breakage.

▶ Or, the cloth becomes stuck so tight inside the mast that the only way to remove it is with a knife.

▶ A crew member can take hold of the fold in the rigging, which mostly occurs at the top of the sail, and pull the sail inch-by-inch out of the insertion groove at the same time the control lines are carefully pulled on.

▶ The furling line of the jib furler can also jam if locking turns form inside the drum. One can effectively avoid this by keeping light tension on the furling line while unfurling the sail, so that the line will be rolled up tightly and evenly onto the drum.

A strap used as a jack line is very stable and has a good grip.

A Nylon-Strap as a Jack Line

When the wind starts to pick up and the waves start to hit harder, it is high time you start thinking about how the crew can be secured while they are working on deck.

Tip

One tried-and-tested way of effectively preventing man-overboard situations is by running a jack line from the stern of the boat up to the bow. Depending on the deck layout, this line is additionally attached to various points, the mast for example. If the jack line runs extensively in the middle, then the danger of a stumbling crew member going entirely overboard is limited by the length of the lifeline, which is attached to the jack line.

But such a jack line also has a big disadvantage: it is round! And this means that it will simply roll out from under anyone who should happen to step on it. The result: the crew member loses balance and falls! And so this line, which was actually meant to provide safety, could become the cause of the overboard situation.

Instead of rope, a stable nylon strap can be used. This strap doesn't roll away under deck shoes and can even be set-up permanently on many yachts. It can be found at accessory dealers. A nylon strap is very strong and can also be used as an anchor line.

Charterers Should Also Use Lazy Jacks

At the beginning of a charter trip, with a (still) unpracticed crew or with a crew consisting of beginners, reefing becomes a problem. For not until the wind picks up does the skipper find that his/her crew members reluctantly totter around on the foredeck for the purposes of reefing or dropping the main. The correct handling of the proper lines never runs as smoothly at the start of the trip. For this reason, charterers as well as charter companies prefer the furling main, because with this one can comfortably reef in and out from within the safety of the cockpit. The loss of speed through the smaller and flatter sail is acceptable in exchange for the increased safety and comfort levels.

With normal sails there is an acute danger of accidents occurring, in particular with regards to the lowering of the mainsail. The ship's hull is dancing heavily in the waves, the boom, if the mainsheet is not set really tight, oscillates wildly over the deck and a load of sailcloth comes down when letting out the halyard while the crew struggles to keep their balance on the slippery deck, trying to flake the main with as few wrinkles as possible. What can one do to improve safety?

The skipper can bring his/her own lazy jacks to the charter trip.

Tip

Here a roll of four- to six-millimeter nylon line from your camping accessories provides the solution as a quickly assembled lazy jack system.

▶ Starting on the port side, for example, a primary line is thrown from the stern side between the shrouds and the mast above the lower spreader with the help of a tied-on tennis ball or something similar.

Someone could of course also be winched into the rig.

▶ The front end is then—now without the ball—secured to the mast at a comfortable reaching height close to the deck. One will surely find a cleat, shackle, or some other possibility for tying on.

▶ The back end is cut off, leaving some 6.5' (2 m) extra length. This end is then tied to the end of the boom or at most one or two meters closer to the mast.

And just like that, our principle lazy jack-line is ready.

Depending on boom length and spreader height, another two or three additional side lines complete our structure. They are tied onto the principle line at similar intervals, led downwards and attached to the boom. Done with the port side! The same thing is done on the starboard side.

Now, while reefing or dropping the mainsail in rough seas, the mainsail will fall between these moderately tight-strung lines and there will be no more mountains of sails on the bucking deck, and the crew is able to safely flake the cloth without wrinkles. When sailing, these lazy jacks can comfortably be brought forward to the mast and secured after having been slacked off. This way, they don't disturb the wind flow or the eyes of the crew. The diversion of this line into the cockpit is, of course, also a practical possibility.

Another benefit: this cheap and simple construction can be safely dismantled and reused on the next charter trip!

Mobile Spinnaker-Sheeting Points

Regatta yachts are usually properly equipped with fittings for the various implementation areas, from trim lines for diverse types of luff and foot, mast bending, sheeting points, etc. On cruising yachts, the selection is often very poor. One either has to be outfitted or mobile aids need to be devised, including spinnaker and gennaker guiding blocks, for example.

Tip

If these guiding blocks aren't already provided near the stern, one can easily install them using the following steps:

Mobile spinnaker-sheeting points can easily be rigged on cruising yachts.

► Attach a short line to a strong, yet inexpensive, single block with a figure-eight knot.
► Pass the resulting loop over a stern cleat in such a way that the block can swing freely, fair of the stern railing, for example.
► Now rig the spinnaker or gennaker.
► Sheet or afterguy are fed through this block and can then be led to a winch in the cockpit.
► For adjustment of this sheeting point, also available, as on a regatta yacht, is a barber hauler (see "DIY Barber Hauler" p. 24).

Thus equipped, there is nothing more standing in the way of the enjoyment of this colorful foresail. With a block brought from home, even the charter skipper can add wings to the genoa of his/her charter yacht.

The guiding blocks quickly and easily disappear below deck or in the aft locker when not in use.

Just One Sheet on the Gennaker with Sock

For cruising sailors, the gennaker is a welcome addition to the sail selection, because it can easily be handled by a small crew and has a wider range of application than the spinnaker. If you supply it with a sock, then the setting and dropping works even better. But the following still has to be prepared: The head is attached to the spinnaker halyard, the tack is attached at the bow (a small gennaker boom would be excellent), and the sheets are individually led aft and there placed on their respective winches. This still takes a little effort. I have deter-

mined that on cruising yachts the gennaker is very seldom shifted and it is also very rare to jibe with this sail. This colorful shoot is usually hoisted when one intends to sail on the same tack for a long period. So why have a second sheet? Which is set up on the windward side and leads to the cockpit, but which usually doesn't get used?

Tip
Personally, I leave out the second sheet and manage with just one on the lee side. And when the need comes for me to jibe, then I first pull the sock over the gennaker, set up the sheet on the new side, change course, and release the colorful sail from the sock on the new tack. This saves time setting up the sail as well as money, since only one line and one block are required.

One line is completely sufficient.

Reefing with a Catamaran

Many skippers aren't fully confident with chartering a catamaran, because sailing on a multi-hull yacht is thought to be different from sailing on a keel yacht. This is not so! A cat also has a jib and mainsheet, a traveler, and the usual trimming devices. However, a multi-hull doesn't indicate the time to reef through heeling, it merely converts the higher wind pressure into speed. (Incidentally: My Tobago 35 does this at a maximum speed of 15 knots).
I have implemented further attempts at increasing speed. Cruising speeds of approximately eight to eleven knots have been achieved with five to six Beaufort. But you can also easily do it yourself here.

Wind pressure is converted to speed.

Tip

The skipper can determine the right time to reef, which is when the wind speed continues to pick up but the cat's speed stops increasing significantly. On well equipped cats, one will also find a reefing diagram where the crew can check which reef is recommended for which wind-speed. This could appear as follows:

Full sails	Up to 16 knots apparent wind
1. Reef	up to 25 knots
2. Reef	up to 35 knots
3. Reef	above 35 knots

Of course, the foresail surface is also reduced correspondingly. Another difference with the mono-hull: when the wind freshens or a squall sets in, with a keelboat one normally heads up, with the purpose of either sailing higher or of letting some pressure out of the rig.

In any case, the yacht then heels over correspondingly. With the cat, on the other hand, one falls off a little, in order to convert the stronger wind into greater speed. One thereby reduces the pressure in the rig and avoids the danger of capsizing. If one would head up, one would increase the sail pressure and since the yacht cannot heel it could broach, the windward hull could lift, and (theoretically) capsize. Generally, it is only the forces in the rig that increase, which is why the standing and running rigging on cruising catamarans are designed to be very stable.

Reefing without a Flapping Sail

Sailing can be such a beautiful thing. Racing along in a fresh breeze, skipper and crew are pleased with the optimal speed. But then the wind increases and it slowly becomes time to reef. The skipper is not quite comfortable with the large amount of canvas or with the small and ill-experienced crew on board, especially when he thinks of how the flapping and raging mass of cloth is to be kept under control during the reefing maneuver.

But there is another way—without noise, without flapping sails, or jib sheets whipping around the ears of the foredeck crew.

Beginners, don't worry if, when reefing, the sail does not beat.

Tip
- ▶ Bring the yacht to a moderately close-hauled course.
- ▶ The traveler stands far to leeward, so that the mainsail is only just filled and still not flapping.
- ▶ The jib is full and keeps the yacht on course and maintains the speed. This is very important, because the helmsman has full control over the yacht during the entire maneuver.
- ▶ One of the crew can now head forward on the scarcely heeled deck (with clipped-on lifebelt) towards the mast.
- ▶ The crew member releases the main halyard and pays out enough so that the reefing cringle can be hooked onto the bullhorn.
- ▶ Now he can reengage the halyard. Even now there is still a little wind in the mainsail. The boom is in the lee (away from your head) and there are no sails flapping in the wind. This is also good for preserving the longevity of the sailcloth.
- ▶ The last step is pulling through the slack of the reefing lines and pulling tight the line of the actual reef. Done!

Nobody has to worry about the traveler or mainsheet during the entire maneuver. The frightful power of the flapping sailcloth, especially for the inexperienced, is completely eliminated, the sail is left untouched, and during all this the journey continues without crashing into the waves and with little heeling. Try it for yourself!

Info: If the halyard or reefing lines are led back to the cockpit, then of course the foredeck man only has to worry about the reefing cringle.

And another tip: If I am on a trip with a small or inexperienced crew, then I put in the second reef directly. Advantage: Only if it really starts to blow hard does one have to go to the third reef and, for me as cruising sailor, the difference in speed between the first and second reef is insignificant compared to the increase in safety.

Roll On, Roll Off... or Not

Having one of these practical roller furling systems has become indispensable on modern yachts. There is hardly a cruising sailor out there who can go without this easy-to-use device. But sometimes it gets stuck!

Tip
- ▶ The least complicated fix is when you need to remove a locking turn from the reefing drum. A crew member has to go onto the foredeck, the pressure has to be taken off the reefing line, and the line has to be untangled—wind by wind. Depending on the weather, this can be a strenuous and wet affair. If that doesn't work, then the furled-out genoa, with the use of a lot of power in strong winds, can be furled around the forestay by hand, using the released sheets—furl by furl.
- ▶ Alternatively, the sail can also be simply dropped: jib halyard off and sail down.

The forestay has to be checked regularly.

A roller furling also ages. This means that individual components wear out, corrode, or fall apart in other ways. The result is that problems arise when furling. Getting mad at the manufacturers won't do any good here either; we have to roll up or pull down the genoa by hand. It is rare, but it has happened before, where the forestay unravels and the drum gets blocked. The forestay is known to be made up of various wires that are twisted around each other, and both ends are inserted into a cable terminal where they are compressed under strong force. On rare occasions it can happen that—as a result of corrosion—one or more of these wires snap off right above the top of the bottom terminal and form cumbersome kinks. These projecting wires are located inside the reefing drum and therefore cannot be seen! They then dig into the surrounding material until they get stuck, blocking the drum. In this case, the only solution is to disassemble the bottom part of the roller furling, release the damaged parts, and temporarily compress the loose wires with binding wire, strong tape, or something similar.

Of course, the forestay is now weakened and cannot carry the full load. Thus, an additional safety, for example the spinnaker halyard, has to be attached to the bow and set tightly in order to take a part of the forestay load.

It is needless to say that the sail area also needs to be adjusted under these conditions.

Rolling Jib Taken at Its Word

Everyone knows that in Australia, a lot of things work differently. Beyond the fact that at midday the sun is in the north, the sailors over there also have different ideas.

In Sydney harbor, there is a catamaran with a rotating rig. This construction comes com-

Here the entire rig is rotated.

With this boomed jib, the jib is rolled into the boom.

Sleep Killers: Halyard and Crew

Ping, slap, boing—every boating enthusiast knows these noises, and (almost) everyone is unnerved by them: slapping halyards are the cause.

Tip

During the day, nobody notices that the main halyard is hanging loose or that the spinnaker halyard isn't properly secured. Only at night, when calm has come over the marina, do these deceitful parts of the rigging start their nerve-racking work. They rattle incessantly and there can be no real thought of a night's rest. The annoyed skipper will (hopefully) get up, crawl on deck, and span the noisemaker away from the mast using strops or other measures, thereby restoring the peace and quiet.

What is surprising is the fact that often, most yachts bob around at their moorings in complete silence and only one yacht has a rattling halyard. The most surprising is that the crew on this vessel is sleeping the sleep of the righteous and doesn't notice a thing. They are, of course, assured the "benevolence" of all harbor inhabitants, because they could easily silence the halyard and then everyone—skipper, crew, and jetty neighbors—could sleep peacefully.

pletely without shrouds; the jib is mounted on a boom, which is connected and flush with the mast.

This is very practical, since—with this rig—one never has to jibe, the entire mast is simply swung around to the front and secured. But the secret here is the furling jib. The owner of this foresail does not furl it around the forestay as is normally done; it is furled into the boom! Just as there are two furling-possibilities for the mainsail—in/on the mast or into the boom—the exact same applies to the foresail. The benefit of this is that the weight of the furled sail lies very low and is not suspended high above deck.

With this adjustment the crew sleeps soundly.

But another yacht crew is perhaps returning from the pub and decides to have a night cap on deck.

Depending on the enthusiasm, this could last until the early morning hours and the noise level may keep the entire marina up. If the levels remain high, appeals or commands about the noise disturbance are ineffective, since they significantly contribute to the sound being created and may further disturb your neighbors. Fortunately, at some point peace returns and the blanket of sleep is slowly pulled over the harbor.

And when all the halyards are finally silenced and the skippers are once more snoozing in their warm bunks, a warm breeze wafts across the marina, and then, yes then, the topping lift softly begins to sing.

Snap Shackles on the Clew and the Tack of the Gennaker/Spinnaker

Spinnaker, kite, gennaker, or whatever they may be called are also very effective light-wind sails for cruising sailors and charter-

A snap shackle on the clew and the tack of the gennaker/spinnaker can be cast off quickly.

ers, which are mostly set on broad-reach or downwind courses.

Despite all the simplifications with specific sail cut or socks, the often small or inexperienced crew regularly has problems keeping the many square feet in check, especially when the helmsman broaches, causing the colorful chute to collapse, become entangled, and get stuck. Since the wind keeps blowing into it while the crew is trying to drop the sail, they cannot manage to subdue the canvas to bring it down. And if the halyard is then significantly released, the entire spectacle flies into the water, quickly making its way beneath the hull to become entangled around the rudder and prop. At this point, it becomes very difficult to recover the large cloth in one piece.

Tip

Here, simple snap shackles on the clew and tack will help, even before anything goes wrong. If the sail becomes entangled or the yacht sways/heels too much, then one can just release the snap shackle and the canvas will blow far to the lee, immediately releasing any pressure from the chute. The sail, yacht, and crew are out of danger once again. One crew member attends the spinnaker halyard and slowly releases it while another pulls in the clew and gathers the sail cloth on deck. Here, the yacht can also be left drifting, so that the helmsman—especially in a small crew—can actively help bring in the sail.

When the Mast is Standing Straight

Many cruising sailors wonder why their yacht sails faster on one tack than on the other, or why the log shows different speeds. This could happen because the paddle wheel is not mounted exactly amidships and, according to the hull position, the paddle will turn at different speeds. The result is a different speed display for courses on the port and starboard tack, although the yacht is sailing at the same speed.

However, another possibility is that there really is a speed difference, which could be the result of the mast not standing exactly upright.

Tip

This can easily be tested using the main halyard. Pulled to one side up to the toe rail—for example, right next to the chain plate—mark the length of the halyard. Measured on the opposite side at the same symmetrical reference point, you can determine whether the mast tends towards the port or starboard side. Note: If the roller of the halyard is not built into the middle of the mast, then the measurement has to be corrected accordingly.

The shrouds can now be tensioned until the spar stands completely vertical. This method is too imprecise for regatta experts. They use a measuring tape, with which they measure up to the exact inch, but the above method suffices for the ambitious cruising sailor.

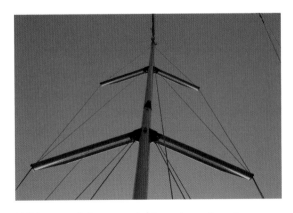

With a straight mast, both tacks sail well.

Completely Off the Hook: The Roller Furling Drum

A furling jib is a great system, seeing as no one has to run around on the foredeck or struggle with piston hanks. The foresail can be set and furled from within the comfort of the cockpit—but only if the system is working properly.

He who isn't careful, risks entanglement.

Tip

▶ Problems can start as early as the mounting and with mast trimming: Too little forestay tension causes the stay, and thus the aluminum fixture of the furling system, to sag. This not only affects the close-hauled performance characteristics when sailing, the furling system will also struggle to turn when it sags.

▶ Another important point is the leading of the furling line. It has to be set up in such a way that the line leaves the drum at a right angle. If this is not done, then the line will be wrapped on one side of the drum and either get blocked or run off the drum's edge. And once again, things will get stuck.

▶ Finally, one can also do something wrong during operation that will lead to seizure. The foresail is, of course, simply furled out using the jib sheet (on the right side!). If one simply allows the furling line to roll up loosely onto the drum, then it will twist and create locking turns or even real knots when it comes to furling the sail. Why? Very simple: because the first winds, which lie very loosely in the furling drum, are compressed by the outer windings. The inner windings cannot handle this: they form loops and finally a blockage. Sorting this out with a sharp knife—on a rolling foredeck—is a thankless and wet affair. It is better to let a second person control the furling line when furling out the jib and to let it be rolled up with a light pressure. Now the windings are tight and even in strong winds the furling presents no problem.

Taking in the Foresail

It is not always easy to furl in the foresail, especially on a close-hauled course. The wind pressure is enormous and so is the force on the furling line, and on the drum. Instead of using brute winching power to furl the sail, there is an easier way.

Tip
The foresail is easier to furl if the helmsman quickly falls off on a broad reach and the sail is then furled. The advantages are obvious. The apparent wind decreases and thereby also the pressure in the sail. If the jib is also covered by the main, then absolutely no wind remains in the sail and it can be furled in or reefed without a great deal of energy. Especially when cruising, the small loss in height plays no role, since safety and problem-free maneuvering are priorities.

The genoa furled away quickly and easily.

If the yacht has a conventional foresail with piston-hanks—without jib furler—then, when it comes to dropping the sail, the jib halyard is simply released as soon as the yacht lies dead into the wind. The advantages: the sail falls on the foredeck instead of in the water and can be easily and safely gathered and tied down by the crew.

It is time to reduce the sail-area.

3. Anchor and Winch

On the Chain

In many bays there are mooring buoys, to which yachts can or must tie on. When one has to tie to mooring buoys and the anchor remains in its locker, it is usually partly because the community wants to open up new sources of revenue, partly for the safety of the yachties, and partly to protect the underwater environment, coral for example. Often, tying on is made easy for the skipper.

▶ Fish the guiding lines with a boat hook,
▶ Pull the mooring cable or chain onto the foredeck,
▶ Tie onto the bow cleats—that's it.

This is fine when the weather is calm. But if a strong wind comes up, it can become impossible to remove the cable or chain loop from the cleat, while the wind makes the yacht strain heftily against the mooring. Only prevention helps here.

Tip

▶ Do not attach the mooring cable or chain directly to the vessel, but use an auxiliary line, or preferably two, for safety.
▶ Pass these lines through the loops of the mooring and slip them back on board as with normal mooring lines.
▶ Do the same with the second line.

Now you can release the yacht from the mooring under any conditions. The groaning and creaking noises are also dampened, which provides for a quiet night. And one more fact: If the chain comes into contact with the hull during a wild ride, this could result in deep chafing marks in the bow. Owners and charter companies love this.

Well secured to the buoy.

Incidentally: Many areas have their own special features. In the Baltic Sea there are moorings and pilings, in the Mediterranean and overseas, anchorage and tying onto moorings is more prevalent, and many times there are buoys ready for yachts.

Plucking-out the Anchor by Hand?

When the yacht is at anchor, it is very desirable for the anchor to be dug in deep and holding rock solidly. But when it comes to pulling the anchor back up, one wants the iron to let go of the bottom.
But this doesn't always happen, for example when the anchor is stuck in thick mud, as if with suction cups or when it is

caught on a rock. If it is a gigantic rock, then only a diver can help. In many other cases, one can recover the chunk of metal by using the measures described here:

Tip

▶ The least amount of force acting on the anchor and chain occurs when one pulls on the chain or anchor rope with mere muscle power. And often it's the sailor's vertebrae that move instead of the metal on the bottom.

▶ A multi-member crew can combine their body weight. For this purpose, as many members as possible move as far forward to the bow as possible—with this weight the bow is pushed down a few inches into the water. The anchor is then pulled as tight as possible and tightly secured. When the crew now moves to the stern, the bow is lifted a few centimeters and so is the anchor. The process is now repeated and at some stage the anchor will (hopefully) be freed.

▶ Even a mechanical or electrical anchor winch will sooner or later reach its limit, but the force that one can apply with it is already enormous, and one has to consider whether the rest of the yacht, the cleats, the bow fitting, or the winch foundation itself can handle this force without breaking.

This is great for the lower back.

▶ Caution is required when one tries to pluck out the anchor with mechanical help. Many crews give a lot of gas so the yacht shoots over the anchor to lift the anchor shaft and thus break the anchor free. This often works very well, but if one gives too much gas and the anchor is truly stuck tight, one could quickly rip out the whole anchor winch or the bow fitting from their mountings and watch them sink.

Anchor Locker Safety

Usually the anchor locker on a sailing yacht is closed with a cover from the top. This closes flush with the deck so that there is no tripping hazard on which to hurt one's toes. This cover is closed with a latch, so that it cannot open accidentally.

If a crew member wants to work with the anchor equipment, the locker cover is opened and should be secured from accidentally closing. Also, just a small gust can blow the cover over, and if your toes are in the way.... That is why the anchor locker cover should definitely be well secured when it is leaning open against the stanchions.

Tip

A simple strop is enough to secure the flapped-open cover. One can use either a short line that is 0.25" to 0.3" (6 to 8 mm) in diameter or a bungee cord. This strop is permanently strapped to the bottom part of the cover, so that it cannot get lost and is always ready for use. The free end is tied to the railing with a clove hitch, or even attached via a small hook which is permanently mounted. Thus, both hands are free to work with the anchor equipment and the anchor locker cover is secured against falling over and shutting.

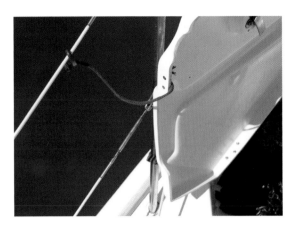

This is the only way to avoid bruises.

a short iron rod no longer helps. It is best to use a strong hook, with which you are able to pull on the heavy iron chain.

▶ Those who don't want to lay on their stomach on the deck in order to reach into the locker can lengthen the hook using a stable rod. Then, the crew member can comfortably guide the anchor chain from a standing position. On mega-yachts, this happens automatically. There is a ready-made mechanism below the anchor winch that, similar to a lawn-sprinkler, makes a slow oscillating movement, thereby avoiding the dreaded chain heap.

Anchor Chain Deployment

Only on larger yachts will one find an anchor locker that is deep enough so that when raising the anchor the chain is evenly divided in the chain area and doesn't create a chain heap which is high enough that it could reach the winch and block it. When this happens, things get stuck, because in most cases the chain has tangled itself so tightly that only brute force and a powerful beating with a hammer can undo the steel tangle. One who wants to avoid this has to fair the anchor chain into the chain locker manually, whether they like it or not.

Tip
▶ When fairing the anchor chain into the chain locker, do not use your hands, the chain is dirty and using your hands is not safe. Instead, use a rod or similar device.
▶ Using the manual winch handle of the electrical anchor winch, you can reach the incoming chain below the winch and guide it into the locker.
▶ When the chain becomes heavier—this mostly occurs with larger yachts—then

Well-stowed means problem-free anchoring.

Anchor Control

In many boating areas of the world, daily anchoring is a recurring chore. It is very important that the hook is holding well, for only then can you sleep peacefully. Despite all the procedures for ensuring that the anchor digs in well, the skipper often still has uncertainty on whether the anchor has a good hold. With a sea bottom such as seaweed, the perceived holding power can sometimes be deceptive. So why not mix business with pleasure?

Tip

In warm areas there is nothing better than jumping in the water for a cooling swim after completing an anchor maneuver. If a snorkel, diving mask, and flippers are at hand, the skipper or a crew member can now follow the anchor chain from the bow of

Seeing is believing.

the ship to the anchor. The underwater visibility in many anchorages is so good, that even a anchor lying 30 feet deep can still be seen clearly.

If the anchor is lying on the bottom and is not, or only partially, dug in, then improvement is necessary. The snorkeler can observe the maneuver from where he is or even direct it. The experienced can even dive down and bury the anchor by hand. Those who have diving equipment on board and know how to use it are well away. They can dive down quite comfortably and secure the anchor equipment at their leisure.

Anchor Watch with Second Anchor

The skipper and crew's sleep can not be disturbed! That is how many boating enthusiasts would like it to be. But when lying at anchor, this requirement is not always feasible. Often, the weather situation isn't calm enough to be able to get away without an anchor watch. An "alarm" for a dragging anchor is a great thing and can be created easily.

Tip

▶ Perform the anchor maneuver as usual. Thus: head to wind, slow movement backwards, and down with the anchor equipment.

▶ Parallel to this, let down a small folding grapnel on a separate line.

▶ Now let out the anchor chain to the desired length and dig in with the motor.

▶ Secure the end of the second line on board. It should hang loose and have no strain.

▶ Tie a bucket to this line and place it on deck.

In such calm weather one can sleep nice and safely on anchor.

▶ Place stones, shoes, or whatever else is available in the bucket. Position and content of the bucket depends on how lightly the crew sleeps.

If the main anchor then slips and the yacht drags, then the line of the smaller, secondary anchor pulls tight and causes the bucket to fall down/over.
Depending on the bucket's contents and the height of the fall, this can cause a hell of a lot of noise—the crew is immediately awakened from their peaceful sleep.

Braked Anchor Winch

Single-handed sailors often struggle with the "Mediterranean" mooring required in many marinas: anchor on the bow and to land with the stern lines. But there are remedies.

Tip
An alternative to the "Mediterranean" mooring is done with the help of the "braked" anchor winch.

Using the braked anchor winch, experienced sailors can execute a solo mooring.

the throttle back to "idle reverse." Hereby, the chain remains taut but the yacht doesn't move any further into the gap; it remains in the same place.

► Now the skipper can quite comfortably go ashore and secure his/her own lines.

► Back on board he goes to the bow, tightens the chain nut, and—with the help of the winch—puts tension on the anchor chain.

The yacht is now tightly secured and the motor is no longer necessary. Of course, there are also remote controls for the anchor winch, with which one can comfortably operate from the helm. But often the switch fails or the laying of the required cables, which are truly thick, is too costly. And many yachts have bow thrusters, which make maneuvering and mooring even easier.

Coiling Thick, Long and Heavy Lines on the Winch

The coiling of various lines on board can be done using various techniques. The important thing is that the coiled line is ready for use quickly—it should not be twisted or get tangled with knots when being thrown to land, for example.

Tip

Thinner rope can be held in the hand and laid on loop by loop, until you finally knot the end so that the line bundle doesn't come loose. Thicker lines are too heavy to be held in the hand. One could lay them on the deck in loops, or a more practical and uniform way is to coil them over a winch. The line is looped onto the winch, coil for coil; use your free

► After preparing the fenders and the stern lines on both sides as well as on the stern, the single-handed skipper maneuvers the yacht in front of the designated berth and turns the hull in such a way, so that when he/she heads back slowly he/she will head straight into the gap.

► Release the anchor chain and let out enough chain so that the anchor will make good bottom contact.

► Now engage the brake on the winch carefully with fingertip precision as far as the yacht, when in slow reverse (thus with "idle reverse"), comes to a standstill and no more chain is let out.

► But if the solo sailor should give throttle, then the anchor will take just as much chain as is pulled out. In this way, a single sailor on board can also maneuver into the gap and then, when there is only about a meter left to the dock, he can take

Use a winch to coil heavy lines.

▶ For this maneuver you need some kind of thin control line that should reach the cockpit.

▶ Push a bight of the line through the anchor shackle or through the chain, about 3.25' (1 m) from one end.

▶ Make a half-hitch using the short end and the bight which was pushed through.

▶ Then hang the anchor over the bow roller as usual, so that when it is dropped it will pull the anchor chain from the chain locker with its weight.

▶ The short end of the line is tied to a cleat, for example. The complete weight of the anchor is now hanging on this line—the chain is loose and ready to be released.

▶ One can now sail to the anchoring spot, and when the time comes, the skipper pulls the control line from the cockpit. The half hitch with a slip is released and the anchor drops into the deep!

hand to control uniformity. The line bundle is tied up as usual using the end. All crew members can coil heavy and long lines in this way.

Remote Starter for the Anchor

Those who have been sailing solo surely know the problems with anchoring and anchor control. The fortunate ones have electric anchor winches with forward and reverse gears that can be controlled from the cockpit. But most skippers won't have such a valuable device on board. Fortunately, there are other ways.

Tip

You can easily anchor by yourself with some kind of a remote starter, a remote release for the anchor.

A remote starter for the anchor—ideal for solo sailors.

In this way the solo sailor (or the skipper with inexperienced crew) can elegantly perform his/her anchor maneuver without running to and fro between the anchor locker and the helm.

Curses and Blessings of the Electric Windlass

Such a device is indeed practical. Simply press the button on the remote control, which shows an arrow pointing up, or the one with the arrow pointing down, to have the electric motor engage and watch the anchor and chain obey, provided that the skipper has found the often well-hidden location of the winch switch or safety and switched it on.

Even so: Especially in the Mediterranean, where as a rule the Mediterranean mooring is used, thus with bow to the anchor and the stern to the dock, the oh-so practical electric windlass is a safety-issue. Why? Very simple, because it releases the chain too slowly. The problem comes from the fact that the anchor should fall in the location that the skipper has envisaged. This is easier said than done when the yacht, as is customary with many modern-day charter yachts, has an electric windlass with up-and-down function, since a normal winch has a release capacity of 1.3' (0.4 m) of chain per second. This means that when the skipper shouts "drop anchor," then the anchor traveling to a depth of 30' needs a whopping 25 seconds before it touches ground for the first time!

By then, a slowly reversing yacht is already against the dock wall and the anchor is lying directly in front of the bow!

Anchoring through the touch of a button.

Tip

Neither an earlier shouting of the command, the timing of which can only be guesstimated—which means that the chain is eventually a few meters short—nor a short stop of the yacht until the anchor touches the bottom—in which case a large heap of chain is often left on the anchor—are good remedies. The helmsman then also has the difficult task of maneuvering the yacht from standstill—there might also be a side wind blowing backwards into the desired berth.

The solution is that the man at the helm slowly reverses in the direction of the berth. The man on the foredeck, at the windlass, releases the winch brake on the skipper's command. The anchor gear falls quickly and nearly directly onto the desired location on the sea bottom. If, during the rest of the maneuver, the chain is moderately released by means of the windlass brake, then the stabilizing effect of the lightly tensioned anchor chain can be utilized and the berth can be directly steered into.

Bridle Spring for Anchoring and Mooring

A bridle for the anchor is normally only found on catamarans, which by nature do not sway around as much when at anchor. But such an additional line can also be very helpful on a keel yacht, since in many harbors there are mooring buoys with which to secure the yacht, but often the angle of pull just doesn't fit. This means that the yacht is lying with its stern to the pier, but the mooring buoy doesn't lie at a precise right angle, so it pulls the yacht a little askew. This isn't pretty and could also be dangerous if one corner of the stern comes too close to the pier. With one additional line, an effective bridle can be improvised. Here's how it works.

Tip
Tie a bowline around the mooring line and let this slide down as far as needed or, if possible to the buoy. If this line is pulled

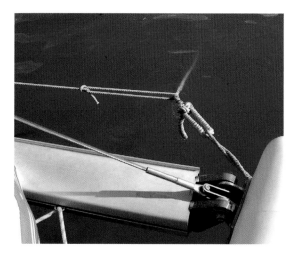

This bridle also tames agile yachts.

tight at a wide enough angle, then the loose bight does not slip back up. But in case it does, one could tie a rolling hitch around the mooring buoy line. When you tighten up the additional line, then this, together with the mooring buoy line, forms a bridle. If this is pulled on, then the angle of attack between the mooring buoy and the yacht changes and thus its position in relation to the pier also changes accordingly. This trick can also help to keep the yacht in a 90-degree angle to the pier, in case of a strong side wind.

Is the Anchor Holding or Not?

The not-very-experienced but responsible skipper in particular asks this question with every anchor maneuver. By observing a few tips, securing the anchor becomes child's play.

Tip
▶ With open anchoring, approach the anchor location head to wind.
▶ When performing a Mediterranean mooring in a side wind—as is customary in the Mediterranean—drop the anchor slightly to windward of the berth, but not on the other side of your neighbor's chain!
▶ The chain should not fall on the anchor. This is avoided by first sailing a little over the desired location, then going into a slow reverse and dropping the gear while moving. The anchor and the chain thus lie in a neat line in front of the bow.
▶ When enough chain has been let out (I let out as much as I can, because the electric windlass easily pulls the weight back in), the maneuver isn't finished yet! The anchor is still lying loose on the bottom. It still has to be dug in.

He who anchors well, sleeps well, too.

way, and are quickly broken. Here you can create a holder for the rail, the stern, or on the engine mount, from which the anchor is easily lifted and immediately ready for use.

Tip

When it comes to purchasing, it doesn't necessarily have to be an outrageously expensive accessory from a marine outfitter—the hardware store around the corner also has a few things on the shelf for the yacht owner. A simple drainage pipe is a useful item for solving our problem. This is rather inexpensive and available in various shapes and lengths. Depending on the size of our folding anchor, we will need a pipe that is approximately 8" to 12" (20 to 30 cm) long, into which we can stick the anchor; it should either fit snugly in the pipe or be stopped by a cap attached to the bottom of the pipe. This pipe can be screwed to a stanchion with stainless steel pipe clamps (not from the hardware store!)

▶ Let the boat drift back with the wind until it starts to hang on the chain, then engage reverse and slowly and carefully (!) increase the revolutions up to around cruising speed. At the same time, take a bearing on two landmarks on the beam that are as far from each other as possible, in order to see if the yacht is still moving. This simulates strong wind pressure on the anchor gear. If the yacht now firmly remains in place and the bearing remains steady, the skipper can relax and enjoy his/her after-maneuver drink.

Bracket for a Folding Anchor

A folding anchor often finds use on sailing dinghies and smaller boats, and of course also on the tender. All these boats have little space and things lying around on the bottom make it look untidy, are generally in the

Tidy equipment.

or to the engine mount with a screw and washer. A second drainage pipe attached next to the first one can hold the anchor line. And just like that, there is order on the boat.

Hoisting with Electric Power

Small crews in particular often struggle with setting the mainsail. It often remains neatly folded on the boom, because the crew doesn't want to go through the effort of hoisting up the big cloth.

Tip

On many yachts, it is possible to rig a system where one can hoist the main using the anchor winch! Either the halyard can be lead directly to the windless capstan or an appropriately placed block leads the halyard to the winch.

A winch with a horizontal capstan has somewhat of an advantage over a windlass with a vertical construction, since the lead of the halyard is simpler. But with appropriate positioning of the block for relaying the halyard, practically any mainsail can be hoisted with the help of the electric windlass.

Chain on the Hook

Tip

Many cruising sailors use a so-called snubber. This is a metal hook which, when lying on anchor, is attached to the anchor chain and then attached to the deck by a line.

An electric winch saves a lot of effort.

A metal hook, attached to the anchor chain, takes the load off the windlass.

This hook takes the load off the anchor chain, the winch is no longer loaded, and chain noises, which can occur at the bow fitting when swinging, are eliminated. If a relatively thin line is used for the attachment of the snubber, then it will break with a loud snap when there is a strong tug on the chain, thus, when a strong wind comes up and drags the boat. This is the wake-up signal for the skipper to get up and check on the wind, weather, and yacht.

Topless Cannister

Sailors in the northern climes often set the example: Instead of the "Mediterranean" mooring (reversing with the stern to the pier) they simply sail forwards when mooring and cast the stern anchor.

The disadvantage of this method is that the stern anchor is usually lighter than the bow anchor, and thus has less holding power; it therefore has to be tensioned by hand instead of using an anchor winch. Furthermore, one also has to climb over the

A lot can fit into a jerry can that has been converted into a vessel.

pulpit in order to get to shore or back on board. The big advantage of this mooring is that the helmsman can control the anchor line himself. The only problem is: Where do you store this bulky stern anchor when sailing?

Tip

If you stow the anchor in the stern locker, it's easy to bring in a lot of dirt and moisture and the handling is cumbersome. One great idea is to attach an opened jerry can to the stern pulpit for storing the anchor gear. Install it outboard and drill a few drainage holes in the bottom so that any collected water or accompanying harbor dirt simply drains overboard.

As anchor gear, the best has proven to be a not-too-light Danforth anchor with at least 16' (5 m) of heavy chain as chain lead, as well as at least 98' (30 m) of anchor line. An anchor line with an incorporated lead line is an advantage. A nylon strap that is rolled onto a drum is also very break-resistant, although not as comfortable to handle as a round line. Anchor, chain, and line should fit into this jerry can. The end of the anchor line should always be safely secured somewhere on board! If, after extensive use, the can starts to show signs of wear and tear, then a new and inexpensive jerry can anchor holder is available at your marine outfitter.

Peacefully Lying at Anchor

A keel yacht just can't keep still. When lying at anchor, it steadily sways back and forth and sails alongside the anchor chain from one side to the other in the anchorage— sometimes so actively that one has difficulty catching it with the tender when returning from land.

This is already annoying enough for the crew on board, but in a popular anchorage, when the yachts are lying tightly packed, it becomes really dangerous and the possibility of colliding with another yacht is not to be ignored.

Tip

▶ Many ketches can be controlled by sheeting the reefed mizzen tightly amidships. This measure stabilizes the ship's hull in the wind and the swinging stops.

▶ With a sloop, take a page from the multihulls: On catamarans, as mentioned before (p. 55), an anchor bridle is connected to the anchor chain in order to eliminate the swinging. Depending on the yacht size, both ends of an approximately 20' to 33' (6 to 10 m) long line are attached to the two bow cleats. This line is shackled to the anchor chain right in the middle of the line and the chain is then slackened until the entire load is carried by the bridle. This moves the pivot point of the yacht a few meters forward and thereby reduces the uncontrolled "swinging."

▶ This method can also work on keel yachts. The length of the line and the optimal attachment points on board can vary from yacht to yacht. Here experimentation is called for!

▶ Another option for stabilizing an anchored yacht when the approach angles of wind and waves are different, is the following trick: A line is shackled onto the anchor chain around 16.5' to 20' (5 to 10 m) ahead of the bow.

The other end is attached to a stern cleat with an adjustable length. Using this bridle, the yacht can be set diagonally to the wind. This makes sense when turning the yacht to face the waves, since one can clearly feel the difference in the rocking compared with the former diagonal pass-

Some yachts are just very difficult to subdue.

ing of the waves beneath the rump, and the crew can get a much more peaceful night's sleep.

Sometimes a secondary anchor is also set in order to keep the yacht in position in a tight anchorage.

Special Hooks for Anchor Clearing

In southern areas as well as overseas, anchoring represents the most-used method of securing the yacht. This is not necessarily the case in the Baltic Sea, where sailors don't often anchor in bays for swimming or in order to overnight. But certainly where "Mediterranean" mooring with bow anchor and stern lines are usually used, anchorage is necessary. Thus, an anchor tangle is pretty much inevitable, because not everyone drops his/her anchor exactly in the planned location.

Instead, the anchor chains lie crisscrossed over each other. At departure in the morning, many yacht crews, despite the electric anchor winches, struggle to raise the heavy anchor gear for untangling.

Anchor tangle, everything but a rarity.

Tip

Because of the weight, the crew will hardly manage to get the tangle high up on deck. The tightly tensioned anchor chains also complicate the hoisting. But one always manages to raise the tangle high enough to be able to see the mess through the water, and it is then that the special hook comes into use.

This hook has a special feature: Two lines are tied to it in a similar way. One lets the hook down until it can take hold of the foreign chain from below. The first line is pulled tight and secured on board. One now slackens one's own chain until it comes loose from the foreign chain. The foreign chain now hangs with your weight on the snubber.

One's own anchor is now hauled on deck or at least kept well clear of the foreign chain. A powerful tug on the, until-now, slack second line on the special hook tilts this in such a way that the foreign chain slips loose and sinks to the bottom.

The yacht is free and can sail off without the crew having done too much.

Every skipper has an uneasy feeling when he knows that another chain is lying over his/her anchor, because if an emergency

departure becomes necessary, the chain chaos will first have to be sorted out. This is aggravated under conditions such as squalls and rain! The yacht can then easily become unable to maneuver and out of control and damage will be inevitable. It is therefore useful for the skipper to indicate the position of his/her own anchor to his/her neighbors when they are performing their anchor maneuvers. Unfortunately, a few skippers ignore such helpful gestures and even lay their chain diagonally across three or four of their neighbor's anchors. In this way the whole harbor is kept busy.

Incidentally: The chain-catching hook can easily be made by an experienced do-it-yourselfer. All one needs are two welded-together and drilled flat irons.

Clearing Locking Turns on the Winch

In strong winds, one has to work quickly and attentively with a winch. The foresail has to go on the other side, and as fast as possible, so that the valuable canvas isn't worn out by unnecessarily flapping in the wind and so that the sail can quickly start providing driving force on the new tack. The maneuver is prepared: The helmsman announces the coming maneuver, the tight-set jib sheet is made clear for quick release, and the still-loose new jib sheet is placed on the winch, ready for sheeting in.

The helmsman now turns the wheel and the yacht swiftly turns through the wind. Once the pressure is out of the sail the jib sheet is released and then it comes. The new jib sheet should now be sheeted in very quickly, hand-over-hand, and that's when it happens...a locking turn on the jib winch! But that's not all, the foresail then fills with a fresh wind, the sheet suddenly becomes

A locking turn can backfire.

Winch Something!

The handling of a winch on a sailing yacht must be learned. Not only because the sheeting in of the sheets and lines mostly needs to happen quickly, but it also needs to happen carefully, without twists in the line and without the user being injured.

tensioned, and the locking turn quickly develops into a virtually undoable tightly compressed knot! This can be quite danger-ous, since the foresail can now no longer be controlled.

Tip
The situation can quickly be resolved using a knife, but there is also a different way.

► Tie a free line to a rolling hitch ahead of the winch onto the loaded jib sheet.
► Lead this extra line to a free winch and take it up on that winch.
► This takes on the load from the locking turn on the jib winch, which can now be easily released.
► Once this has been done, the jib sheet is taken up on the jib winch as normal, and the rolling hitch can be removed. Sheet, jib, and also the yacht have been saved.

Taking out the twist makes the winch markedly faster.

Tip

Therefore, a few things need to be considered:

▶ First of all, everyone needs to know that the line must always go on clockwise, thus around to the right (when looking at the winch from above). There are only a few yachts where the winches on the port and starboard sides turn in different directions.

▶ Now one needs to make sure that the line is wound around the winch cylinder in even, next-to-each-other and not over-one-another "rings" at least three to four times. This prevents the so-called "locking turn," which is very difficult to undo and can quickly lead to a dangerous situation.

▶ If there is a self-tailing winch on board, then the line which has been wound around the winch cylinder is first led over the "feeder arm" and then wound and pulled tight into the tailing ring. This ring then grips the line and you no longer need to pull on the line in order to ensure that it doesn't slip on the winch, making all the cranking in vain.

Winch Handle with Lock

The most common winch handles being used on sailing yachts today come with a locking mechanism that ensures that they remain securely on the winch and don't go overboard accidentally. But the proper engagement of such a winch handle doesn't seem to be very easy.

Tip

The winch handle with lock has a small lever on the top that is used to disengage the locking mechanism. Before you engage the winch handle on the winch, you have to push the lever to one side in order to disengage the locking mechanism. Now one can engage the handle. Once this has been done, the small lever is released and the handle is locked on.

To remove the handle one does the opposite: First press the lever to the side in order to disengage the lock, and then remove the winch handle without the use of force. Unfortunately, the handle is often forced in when being engaged. The result is that the handle is often so tightly locked that it cannot be removed or that the locking lever of the handle is broken off. A new winch-handle with lock is then required.

The locking-lever must be used.

Deploying the Secondary Anchor

It is sometimes necessary for the crew to deploy a secondary anchor. The reason could be that the main anchor is not holding well, the wind may have turned, or the yacht has run aground and needs to be hauled out.

Tip

The following is required in order to deploy this anchor:

▶ The tender with paddles and perhaps an outboard engine,
▶ One or two crew members in the dingy,
▶ Secondary anchor with chain lead, and
▶ lots of long line.

Start with the line. Tie the end, which will end up on board the yacht, to the tender. The long line is then laid out on the bottom of the dingy in order to run fair, so that it doesn't get twisted during the maneuver. If you have to attach another line, use two interlocking bowlines. Place the anchor chain on the rope heap, and finally position the anchor on top.

If well prepared, the maneuver can be performed in minutes.

This method prevents tangling when the anchor is heaved overboard and sinks into the depths. Once prepared, the tender sets off and travels to a position that is further away from the yacht than the anchor should end up. As the tender slowly travels back towards the yacht, raise the secondary anchor onto the stern mount and, upon reaching the desired anchor position, let it down into the water. The chain and line follow.

When the tender finally reaches the yacht rail, the tender crew hands up the anchor line to the deck and the yacht crew can haul the secondary anchor tight.

This technique has a big advantage over the version where the anchor line is attached to the yacht from the start, in that the small dingy is fully maneuverable and isn't hampered by the long line in the water.

A variation on this method is that the anchor alone travels in the tender and the chain and rope is let out from the yacht. Thanks to the weight of the chain, the tender struggles to reach further than 10' to 15' from the yacht, when it is pulled back by said weight. Even the strongest paddler can't move the tender forward any further.

4. Tender and Outboard

Tightly Strapped on Deck

It is not only the dinghy that is often laid on deck and lashed down during the trip, but also other equipment items such as surf-boards, boat hooks, and gangway planks. In calm weather these items remain where they belong, but when the wind picks up, the waves become higher and spray water comes pouring over the deck, which loosens the lashings. The equipment then runs the risk of coming loose completely and being washed overboard.

Often, the cause isn't limited to the fact that wet ropes become softer, something regatta sailors use to their own advantage with regards to better handling; it lies in the fact that wet rope also stretches. That's why our carefully and tightly lashed tender suddenly comes sliding across the deck. But this negative effect can be turned into a positive!

The dinghy sits firmly on deck.

Tip

Before above- or even below-deck equipment is firmly lashed down, take the lines used for the task at hand and wet them thoroughly. Then carefully lash the items down.

When the ropework dries, it shrinks a little and sets really tight. And in wet weather the lashing, which was already tightened when wet, remains strong.

Going Ashore with the Tender

The sea isn't always calm and without surf, and the shore doesn't always lie protected behind a breaker. Those who still want to undertake the escape to the beach, despite the rougher weather, have to be prepared to use a special technique. But know that even if going ashore goes quite well, the return to the anchored yacht against breaking swell can turn into a true adventure. There won't be any dry feet here.

Tip

First, anything that should not get wet must be sealed in a waterproof container like a dry bag. Protect sensitive items, such as cameras, by placing them in an additional bag before stowing them in the dry bag. It is also advisable to wrap a thick towel around the dry bag.

On many beaches of the Seychelles, where the powerful swells of the Indian Ocean break, the locals have created their own special method for landing that keeps the boat and crew surprisingly dry both when landing as well as when heading back to sea. Here, the dinghy skipper positions himself with his/her boat around 165' (50 m) away from the shore, thus outside of the breaker-zone.

He waits for a higher swell and then gives full throttle. Up on top of the wave he sails towards the beach and slides up the beach along with the wave.

Shortly before the engine propeller digs into the sand and the boat goes aground, he swings the engine shaft out of the water

Those who aren't careful will have wet pants.

dragged into the water as fast as possible and with the bow to the front. The steerer jumps in, swings down the engine shaft in deep enough water and gives gas, in order to move through the breaker zone quickly. As soon as the boat is in the water, the crew also jump in. Everything depends on the right timing: wait for the right wave to break, get the driver in, start the engine, get the crew in, accelerate, and their off!

If this doesn't go smoothly, a wave will break over the tender and fill it up in no time. Then, the crew will neither get the dingy high up onto the beach nor back to the yacht.

Bailing won't help either, because the next wave will follow immediately. Therefore, in such conditions, the skipper really has to strongly consider whether he should grant his/her crew approval to abandon ship, or whether it might be too dangerous.

Sometimes, it really is much easier to just swim to shore—preferably with swimming-trunks, snorkel, and diving goggles.

Securing the Outboard

On many yachts today, there is an outboard motor for the tender, which greatly simplifies its operation. Gone are the days of tedious paddling from the anchorage to the shore—when this little engine starts up dutifully, it effortlessly moves the crew to shore. But one should always secure the outboard against theft, since these items mean quick money or a nice new item for a ne'er-do-well's own boat.

Tip
There are many different anti-theft devices available on the market, but with most outboards a simple padlock will do when

and shuts off the motor at the same time. Pre-positioned helpers await the boat on shore and pull it, still with the help of the wave and as high as possible, up the beach and thus out of the reach of the next wave. The passengers can then climb out—they should emerge rather dry. Returning to the yacht works similarly: When a larger wave shoots up the beach, the dinghy is

it comes to securing the engine against theft, both for safekeeping on board as well when in use on the tender.

Most outboard motors have two toggles on the attachment bolts; using these, the engine mount is clamped on by hand. Usually, there are already holes drilled through the ends of these toggles. If not, you can easily modify these using a small drill bit. Now fold these toggles towards each other in the middle, and you should be able to thread the U-bolt of a padlock through both the holes. If the padlock is now pressed shut, the fastening bolts can no longer be turned and thus the motor cannot be removed. The padlock, as with any moving metal parts that are exposed to the elements, should be treated with a silicone spray from time to time to maintain the mechanism in a working condition.

In the right side of the opposite photo you can see a safety line. This is needed when transferring the outboard from the yacht to the tender. One crew member passes the motor to the second person in the tender, while a third person holds the safety line in hand as assurance. If something goes wrong and the motor escapes the grip of either of the two crew members, then this safety line will prevent a bath or even a total loss of the expensive item.

Another tip: There are also padlocks with very long U-bolts available. One can use such a lock if the fastening bolts are far apart from each other. The important thing is that you shouldn't be able to turn the fastening bolts, because then the opportunist cannot remove the outboard from its bracket on board nor from the back of the tender.

An outboard isn't a must in every area, in some regions one regularly moors in harbors or marinas, and in other places the yacht is not far from the shore.

A strong padlock secures this valuable item.

A Hoist for the Outboard

On the transom of many cruising yachts one can see a small "crane." In most cases this mechanism is attached to the stern railing and serves the purpose of lowering the outboard motor from its mounting on deck down to the tender with very little effort. Besides the substantial weight that such a motor brings into the equation, its awkwardness creates additional difficulties when it comes to lowering the device to the dinghy or raising it again after use.

Many skippers cannot manage it purely because of the required force, and when the yacht and the tender are sloshing around

A outboard hoist secures the valuable item and is very efficient.

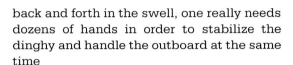
back and forth in the swell, one really needs dozens of hands in order to stabilize the dinghy and handle the outboard at the same time

Tip

The outboard hoist is the proper aid to solve this problem.

For this purpose, a sturdy tubular frame should be mounted on the stern pulpit in such a way that the crane arm can be swung over the outboard in its deck bracket as well as outboard over the tender, which has been secured alongside the stern. A purchase system is attached to the outer end of this crane arm which will take the load.

The skipper prepares the engine for the hoisting operation by rigging a harness around the motor housing using lines or straps. Tie an eye or a shackle to the top of the harness, to which the hoisting mechanism will later be attached. This arrangement can remain on the motor permanently. Once the purchase system has been attached to both the crane and the motor, lift the engine from its bracket. Then swing the crane outboard over the drifting tender and ease the line to slowly let the motor down.

This can even be done by a single person. The crew member who is standing or kneeling in the dinghy can let the outboard down towards himself or hoist it back up to the deck with an effort that is determined by the ratio of the purchase.

You can also use a cleat or a cam cleat for quickly securing the line in the appropriate location, fixing the load at the desired height. You can provide an extra level of safety by making the purchase line just long enough so that even if the motor slips, it cannot fall into the water. Incidentally, other loads can also be lifted from the dingy to the yacht or vice versa using the hoist, including heavy shopping baskets as well as bottles of water and crates of beer.

The Tender on a Long Leash

In many anchorages it is customary to secure motorboats as well as sailing yachts with the bow anchor and one or even two additional long stern lines tied to a tree or rock on shore. In the Mediterranean and the Caribbean, this maneuver is practiced to save space, as it eliminates free-swinging anchoring. But, of course, the ship is not lying directly on shore, so the tender is needed for transfer to land. Although the distance between the stern and the shore is usually only around 30' to 60', getting to preferably managed with dry feet.

Tip

In order for the crew to have the tender at their disposal at all times—whether on board or on land—the tender can be attached on both ends using a continuous line. Here a long line is attached to the bow of the tender. This line is preferably led through a block on board. But leading it around a stanchion will also do. It is then led to shore and through a second block which is tied on shore. Also here the loop of the stern line bowline can be used instead, although the friction will be increased. Then the end of the line is attached to the tender once more.

Using this line, the tender can easily be pulled back and forth from yacht to shore and the crew can go to shore or back to the main vessel at any time.

Extra tip: In strong winds, sling the bowline of the tender's painter loosely around one of the stern lines. Thus, the dinghy is additionally stabilized and you can pull yourself along with the mooring line. No paddles are needed.

A long line suffices as a link between the yacht and land.

The Tender Upside Down on Deck

The dinghy is usually responsible for transporting people, animals, and provisions between yacht and shore. But storing it on deck is usually not the best solution. Attached to the cabin roof, it obstructs the forward view and the way to the mast is turned into an obstacle course. If tied to the stern, it blocks access to the swimming ladder and the way to the dock wall is obstructed.

And on the bow, use of the anchor gear could be prevented by the cumbersome tender. But this is exactly where it can provide a valuable service!

Tip

In southern climes, the weather can be comfortably warm, but can also become uncomfortably hot. Especially below deck—where air circulation is minimal—the hatches simply don't allow enough fresh air into the cabin. If we now use a halyard attached to the painter of the dinghy to lift its bow, we can open the hatch lying underneath it and allow fresh air to enter. Here the hull of the tender acts as an air vent while at the same time shades part of the deck surface, acting as an additional cooling aid. If the dinghy is raised at night, then fresh air can also flow into the bow cabin which lies beneath it.

Properly cleaned, the dinghy serves as a rain cover.

The Tender Out of the Water from the Bow

Light tenders, i.e., inflatable tenders without solid bottoms, can comfortably be let down from the railing to the water by two people. But when it comes to heavy dinghies, inflatable tenders with solid wooden or fiberglass bottoms, or solid dinghies, the story is entirely different. Because they are so heavy, they must be balanced on the unfortunate railing and let down while scratching along the side

of the hull. This is a big task for the crew and torture for the yacht's gelcoat.

Tip

Just as the old seafarers used a loading boom for loading and unloading cargo, the modern yachtie can let down and hoist the tender back up using the spinnaker halyard. The spinnaker pole, or even someone's outstretched arm, serves as a loading boom that keeps the tender away from the hull by pushing on the halyard. A second crew member operates the spinnaker halyard using the halyard winch.

One option is to now shackle on the dinghy with its bow fitting and then bring it on board vertically. Many solid tenders are equipped with hanging eyes for hanging them from the davits, but you can also mount these yourself quite easily. The advantage with these is that the tender can be lowered down to the water horizontally. This method is fast, convenient, and energy and material friendly.

On many yachts the dinghy is stored on deck in a different way. A purchase system rigged to the main or mizzen boom is used for this purpose.

Using this method, the tender isn't dragged over the railing.

The Tender on the Davits

It is not possible to hoist the tender onto davits mounted on the stern on all yachts. Sometimes the large swimming platform is in the way, sometimes it's the wind vane, and sometimes it's simply the fact that access to the swimming ladder would be obstructed by a dinghy hanging on deck.

But even if it would fit, there are still a few things to take into consideration.

The longevity of the tender should be of particular interest to the skipper. Often enough, however, the dinghy is hoisted up so far against the davits that the boat hull of a solid boat or the rubber sides of an inflatable will rub against the steel davits. It is easy to imagine how long a dinghy will last if it chafes while at sea.

Tip

Many owners place pieces of cloth or other materials in between, if not to prevent, then at least to minimize the chafing. But the only way to truly extend the life of the tender is by preventing this swinging motion and maintaining a safe distance between the tender, the yacht hull, and superstructure.

First, the tender is only raised up close to the davits. Then two blocks are attached at appropriate positions on the port and starboard side of the stern through which a safety line is pulled from the bow and respectfully the stern of the tender. It is even easier with catamarans because their transoms extend so far. A practical carabiner serves for the connection to the yacht tender and on the stern the line is pulled tight on a cleat or cam cleat. Now the little boat can no longer swing around uncontrollably on the cross axis of the yacht.

Attach two additional safety lines to the midships of the tender via carabiners. One pulls one side of the boat down and the other one pulls the respective side to the top. Two more cleats provide a tight hold to stop the boat from swinging forward and backward. Lashed in this way all axis of the tender are stabilized and chafing against the davits or even the yacht hull is eliminated. Furthermore, when it comes to letting down the tender, the cleats and carabiners can be released very quickly.

Here the tender is easily raised in the davits.

The Dinghy in the Caribbean

In many sailing regions, the divide between the "rich" yachties and the local population is very pronounced. In particular, there is widespread poverty in the southern Caribbean. It is thus inevitable that visiting sailors become an important part of the local economies in these areas. Some locals trade in fruit and souvenirs, others earn a few dollars through services such as securing stern lines or "dinghy-watching."

The dinghy is not always safe and should be protected.

Tip

The crew is well advised, if they contract a guard to keep an eye on the tender or secure the tender/yacht to a palm tree for a small fee, that the dinghy is equipped with a chain, a steel cable, and a padlock.

The local charter companies have already equipped their dinghies accordingly. Outboards are also permanently connected to the boat with a lock. If not, then a nocturnal change of ownership is sure to take place. But the act of such redistribution and nefarious sourcing is not limited to locals! Refugees who find themselves stranded in the Caribbean or other regions with their boats are forced to rely on such measures if they want to survive.

At night, the dinghy can be effectively secured by hoisting it alongside the hull using the spinnaker halyard. When it has been raised horizontally about two feet above the waterline, it is out of the reach of long fingers. A secondary benefit of this rigging is that the dinghy no longer collides uncontrollably with the stern as it usually would due to wind or current. This means that the crew can enjoy a peaceful night without annoying noises or trouble-makers.

If the dinghy isn't tied on, it quickly drifts away.

The Outboard: The Never Ending Story

Quite often, one can observe the crew and skipper of larger yachts, all ready for going ashore, sweating and swearing as they struggle to get the engine for the tender started. Everyone gets a chance to turn and adjust the knobs and levers and to pull on the starter cord until exhaustion. Alas, as the motor relaxes, the irritated, thirsty crew must row to shore.

HydroDock International
305-944-6300

To achieve full power, outboards must be well maintained, like these four 250-hp engines.

Dinghy outboards lead a merciless existence. During the day they are exposed to the scorching sun and at night to the condensing moisture. When sailing, the seawater sprays into every crevice of the outboard and during a crew change and/or before departure, the outboard is tested on its mount outside of the water. As if getting started wasn't hard enough, running the engine without cooling water destroys the rubber impeller of the water pump in minutes! Overheating and engine blockages are the results during its next use on the tender. Usually, the distance between the yacht and shore is so short that the outboard never gets a chance to heat up properly. Many times the engine is started, gunned to full throttle, and then shut off after only traveling 300 feet. The results: poor fuel-efficiency, soot, and a dirty sparkplug.

Even just handing the motor from the yacht deck down to the tender is a life-threatening operation for the outboard. If someone places it upside down, for example, with the propeller higher than the engine block, then the remaining seawater in the shaft runs back into the motor and into the cylinders. The result: it seizes.

And even if the engine is handed over the correct way, the wind and the seaway often turn the operation into a dance party and the outboard heads to the bottom. If it is then recovered, it should actually be dismantled and freed of every trace of salt, but in most cases people just wait until the water has run out and then they immediately try to start it up again—with the same result as described above.

Tip:
▶ Secure the expensive outboard with a safety line when transferring it to the dingy.
▶ Once the engine has started, let it warm up before revving it at full throttle.
▶ From time to time, travel a good distance to give it a thorough cleaning.

▶ Empty the float chamber of the carburetor to prevent the fuel mixture from gumming-up.

▶ Frequently remove all salt from the engine housing and block.

▶ For winter storage, prepare the outboard according to the manufacturer's instructions and store it in an upright position.

Double-Leashed Holds Better

Sailor's knots should be durable, but also easy to undo after use. Especially in the case of varying loads, as is frequently experienced by the painter of the tender, the knot's ability to hold cannot necessarily be guaranteed. It is common to find that a

Those who have lost a dinghy before use double lines.

tender that was secured to a stern or pier has gained its independence and the cause was a knot that had come undone.

Tip

One can additionally secure the sailor's knot with an added whipping or by splicing on an eye splice, but using a second painter as a security measure is still desirable.

Permanently attach this second line to a different location than the normal painter, since vulcanized lifting eyes can also rip out from the dinghy. And just like that, the vessel is gone!

Carabiners spliced on to the painters are also useful, since these can be operated with one hand.

Thus equipped, the chances of the tender gaining its independence are slim.

Maneuvers for Getting In and Out of the Dinghy

Less experienced crew members may encounter real problems when heading to land via dinghy. Just getting into the small tender from the yacht can often cause stress. But there isn't really that much that can happen! In the worst case scenario, one falls in the water and gets wet. But despite this, such situations can and should be avoided.

Tip

With little swell, the maneuver is usually quite simple: The tender is pulled towards the yacht deck and the crew simply climbs into the boat. This is easier if a low-lying swimming platform is available. Only when it comes to climbing down the swimming ladder onto the transom does it become more difficult.

Boarding a dinghy is much easier on the back of a large catamaran.

The maneuver becomes interesting with wind and waves. Then, it's not only the tender that dances up and down, but the yacht is also tugging at the anchor and moving in the swell. Here a misstep can sometimes occur. If the tender is tied on along its side at the stern, the crew will have significantly greater stability. In this way, it cannot be pushed underneath the stern of the yacht. From the swimming platform you can move into the tender sideways with a big step. With eyes to the front, you can hold on to the railing with your hands and perform the maneuver quite securely. The following applies once you are in the boat: Sit down and make space for the next person.

If necessary, the tender can be further stabilized by securing a stern line to the yacht as well.

Getting back on board is just as easy.

Cruising Comfort: Tiller Extension for the Outboard

An outboard on the stern of the tender is fun and considerably expands the range it can cover. The performance of a small dinghy is extremely dependent on the weight distribution of its passengers. This is why one often sees people sitting far forward on the bottom or on the rowing bench of the boat while holding the outboard tiller in an awkward position.

In small tenders there isn't a built-in helm with steering and throttle, but a tiller extension on the outboard motor helps improve general seating comfort, weight distribution, and significantly improves cruising and planing performance.

This is how a well-trimmed tender should sit in the water.

Tip

Tiller extensions of various lengths are available for purchase at most marine outfitters. The tube can also be cut to the required length. The tiller extension is simply connected to the throttle of the outboard via a universal screw mount. In the same way, it can also be quickly screwed off at any time. Many of these devices even have an engine-stop button, as is found on the tillers of more powerful outboards. This comfort shouldn't be renounced; a tender equipped with a tiller extension lies balanced on the water, and with proper weight distribution planing is reached and maintained much quicker than when the dinghy driver has to sit at the stern on one side in order to be able to hold the normal short tiller properly.

Fender as Tender Brake

Storing the dinghy in the davits when not in use is very practical. Here it is well lifted and ready for use in an instant. There is only a question of how the tender is to be secured so that it doesn't rock around wildly when at sea. If the boat is hoisted right to the top, so that it rests against the metal parts, then it will chafe in the contact areas and the outer skin of a rubber boat will quickly be chafed through and start leaking. A solid tender makes unpleasant noises when being scraped.

Tip

If you lash small fenders underneath the metal davits so that they come to lie between the dinghy and metal, then both will be well protected. One might possibly also need thin safety lines in order to control the movements of the tender.

Outboard Harness

On many yachts, the outboard spends a lot of time on its bracket on the stern railing. Here it is raised when not in use. But when it needs to be placed on the back of the tender, things become difficult. Very small engines can still be lifted from the yacht to the dinghy by hand, but with larger motors things become increasingly difficult. And if there is choppy water making the yacht dance around, which in turn makes

A tender can quickly be ruined by chafing.

The outboard is under control.

the dingy dance even more; it may not be possible to attempt mounting the outboard without it winding up in the sea. Of course, an outboard that has taken a bath may not be recoverable.

A safety line tied to the hand grip of the engine and secured by a second person on board may prevent this problem, but the motor hangs horizontally and is thus difficult to handle.

But if you take the trouble to tie a lanyard around the motor head in such a way that the long end of this "double-loop" comes out in the center at the top of the motor cover, the line can be used to vertically lift the engine. The free end of the lanyard is knotted and used as a transportation grip. If the line is long enough, one can even lead it through a block attached to the boom and use this combination as an efficient hoisting mechanism. Many sailors use a wide nylon strap instead of a lanyard. This can be fitted tightly around the motor housing with the use of appropriate tensioning clips. But be careful. The nylon strap and lanyard should only be looped around in such a way that they are not in the way of any movable parts.

What Belongs in the Dinghy?

One often hears Pan-pan reports being broadcast on the VHF concerning missing tenders with one or two people on board. The causes are often a striking outboard, missing paddles, and the underestimation of the wind drift on the open sea. With proper equipment on the yacht tender, such dangerous situations can be avoided.

Tip
When planning an escape with the tender, you should not only inspect the fuel level

of the outboard tank, you should also take a small reserve container. Quite often the problem is a mere lack of fuel. A small emergency supply of gasoline is invaluable in such a situation. Fuel canisters are available at most outdoor sport retailers.

These containers are usually made of lightweight aluminum and are approved for holding fuel.

There should always be two paddles in the boat, otherwise a strenuous swimming trip might be in the cards. A practical folding anchor takes up hardly any space but keeps the dinghy in position and away from sharp coral heads while its occupants go snorkeling. It also helps stop the drag a little if the

With "basic equipment" the dinghy is well prepared.

worst case scenario comes to pass. Used as a stern anchor when going ashore, it keeps the dinghy off the dock wall.

In rough seas a life vest per person can do no harm. Know your local regulations regarding the required onboard safety equipment.

A small sponge is good for cleaning the tender. It can be used to remove small amounts of water from inside the boat. For larger volumes, a bailer is recommended. This can easily be made out of a fabric softener bottle. On longer tender trips, it might also be a good idea to take a mobile phone so that the remaining crew can be contacted if problems should arise. In any case, one should advise the crew remaining on board of your departure and when you have arrived back on board, so that they don't worry.

In warm regions a bottle of drinking water, sunscreen, and a T-shirt could be very handy.

Pilot boat at the Kos Marina.

5. Electric Wiring and Computers

"Protection" for Electric Cables and Water Hoses

Mega-yachts aren't the only vessels that spend long periods of time with a water hose connected to the marina tap and a cable plugged into the dock side power outlet. Practically all cruising yachts have an exterior power cable and the water tanks also have to be filled regularly. In the marina, you'll notice that these supply lines are pulled tight so that the clean cables don't hang in the dirty marina water. The results are that the connectors on the electric cable get stretched to their limit and the water hose can be quickly pulled off the connector, resulting in a flood. However, if the water hose and power cables hang in the water, they quickly become dirty. With power cables, a tear in the insulation can quickly cause a short circuit when coming in contact with water.

The power cable and water hose are well protected from the elements in this sheath.

Tip

Resourceful owners have a sail maker make some "protection." Thin strips of awning fabric, similar to what bimini tops are made of, can be sown into sheaths that are an approximately 1' to 1.3' (30 to 40 cm) wide and several feet long. This protective sock can then be attached to a mooring line with reef knots as with sail ties. One could also sew on Velcro strips for easy closure. Cables and hoses can be loosely enclosed in this protective strip. To prevent dirt from entering this cover, the "protection" can also be sealed along the top edge with Velcro or a zipper.

Digital and Affordable Battery Monitoring

Electronics stores offer a wide range of effective solutions for monitoring the charge level of the on-board batteries. However, the purchase of such a device leaves a significant hole in the budget. Through a favorable property of lead-acid batteries, a viable monitoring of the batteries can be achieved for less than $15.

Tip

A fully charged lead-acid battery will have a voltage of around 12.7 volts with no load. A discharged battery will show a charge of only 11.6 volts. Our goal is to find a suitable and high-resolution voltmeter. Most electronics stores sell affordable, digital voltmeters that display readings with two decimal places. The best place to place the instrument is at the navigation table. Replace any (simple) instruments with the new one. Clamp the new device to the existing terminals.

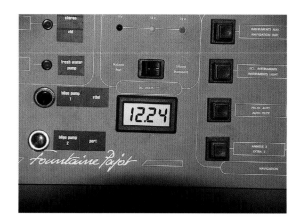

This $15 battery monitor also indicates the charge level accurately.

If no voltmeter is available, locate the positive and negative terminals of the starter and house batteries and attach the measuring device there. In both cases, it is a task that takes little time and can be performed by non-electricians, because only non-hazardous low voltage is involved.

If various battery circuits are to be monitored with a single voltmeter, install a small switch so that batteries can be checked individually.

If you install a separate voltmeter for each battery circuit, you can get a read on all of them at the same time.

Note that if the batteries are being charged by the alternator of the propulsion motor or by the battery charger, other values will be shown. If the battery charge was significantly low and the charging has just begun, then a reading of a little higher than 13 volts is displayed—it will increase as the charging progresses. But with a maximum reading of 14.4 volts, the limit is reached at the so-called "gassing" voltage. If this value is not reached, you may have line losses, voltage dropping due to long cabling. But this doesn't matter, since we are just measuring information about

the condition of the battery. When measured directly at the battery, the voltmeter should read 14.4 volts when a charging device is connected and 12.7 volts for an open-circuit voltage.

While this $15 battery monitor may not satisfy those looking for the highest standards in accuracy, the battery's general status can be easily determined.

The Open-Plan Office On Board

Electronic devices have now become indispensable on yachts. Computers and related technology provide weather information as well as help with navigation and completion of the logbook. Many boating enthusiasts even take some of their office work out of their stuffy office and work on it in the fresh sea air. They are assisted by the usual office technology such as computers, printers, scanners, and external hard-drives. Through mobile technology and wireless networks, the necessary yacht-to-land connection is made via telephone, fax, mail, and the Internet.

All of these devices are easily integrated with each other (as on land), but when it comes to power supply, varying supply voltages can present problems.

Tip
One solution is an inverter, which turns the 12 volts typically available on board to 110/220 volts for consumer electronics. In addition, a gas- or diesel-powered generator provides ample power, but makes a lot of noise.

Luckily, car chargers for laptops and mobile phones also allow direct access to the 12-volt, on-board supply. Many inkjet printers and even scanners can operate with 12 volts using appropriate connectors. Other peripheral devices, such as drives and external burners, often require only five volts and can easily be connected through a switchable voltage divider, available in many auto part stores for connecting small devices.

Information on the required voltage and the way the plug should be poled can be found on the device, right next to the plug.

An external plug-in power supply, which normally converts the power supply to the typical 110/220-volt circuit found in houses, is a welcome device in the search for suitable on-board devices. If such an external power supply is available, one can also see what kind of power the appropriate device requires on the rating plate. Instead of this plug-in power supply, the appropriate connection can then be made to the on-board electrical system.

The dream of working independently from around the world shouldn't remain unfulfilled—even on board.

The Laptop on Deck

The on-board computer has now become indispensable on (almost) all yachts.

Fixed servers on large yachts handle e-mail and Internet connections, monitor on-board electronics, facilitate navigation software, and serve as multimedia servers with many Gigabytes of video and music for the crew's enjoyment. On smaller yachts, the laptop has found its way into the navigation corners—even charterers often refuse to go on board any yacht without their laptop. It may well be very practical, when weather information, e-mails, electronic navigation, and even the logbook can be centrally prepared and saved on the laptop, but who wants to spend part of their well-deserved holiday as a woodlouse in the belly of the ship at the navigation table, while the rest of the crew enjoys the sun on their skin? Unfortunately, laptop screens aren't bright enough so that one can place them in the cockpit to work,

since peering at the dim screen is unbelievable strenuous on the eyes.

Tip

Fortunately, companies have given this some thought and have developed practical laptop tents especially for professional use. Some can fold down to very small sizes and thanks to springs can be unfolded super quickly. Others have dual functionality as laptop bags or backpacks. Protection from rain is another benefit these accessories are capable of. Such products range in price from $25 to $100.

But for the price of a three-ring binder, you can craft your own sun shield. A binder is ideal because it is widely available and the material is relatively stable, but also light. Light plastic or metal sheets can also be turned into shades. The back of the folder is the size of a letter-size page, so the long side fits perfectly for a 15" laptop. Follow these steps:

▶ Cut off the back side of the folder.
▶ Now, cut off the front side so that only the 3-ring mechanism remains—this can go in the bin.
▶ Then, cut the front side diagonally; these will be used to make side panels.
▶ Next, screw U-formed metal brackets to two of the back panel corners. These will attach the shade to the top of the screen.
▶ Now, simply attach the other two side panels to the bottom panel using duct tape. This allows you to fold the side panels together and easily transport the device.

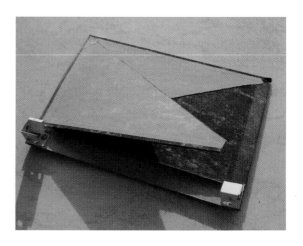

The homemade "PC-shade" described here might not be entirely as effective as its professional counterparts, but it takes around 20 minutes to make and costs practically nothing.

Working in the shade even when the sun is shining on deck.

Voice Recorder for Completing the Logbook

The ship's logbook is not only an important piece of evidence in case of an accident at sea, but it also serves as a reference and reading materials for future sailing. Of course, it needs to include the important navigation and seamanship entries, but the logbook only becomes gripping reading when all the small eventualities—positive and negative—are also included.

But it isn't always so easy to complete the logbook in such detail that it becomes an interesting read, since the rolling of the yacht in rough seas deters many skippers from going down below and putting witty words to paper on a dancing chart table.

Tip

A small dictation device fits in any jacket pocket and is always close at hand. Here the daily events can be recorded quickly and easily. Whether in strong winds at sea or on a bicycle tour of the island, the dictation device can be handled with one hand and record the highlights immediately after they are experienced. And in a quiet hour, the skipper, whether sitting comfortably in the cockpit or in his/her armchair at home, can relive the experience once more and enrich his/her personal logbook with pasted-in photos and text.

Simple and practical, a voice recorder is always close at hand.

Color Coding for Electric Wiring

Every owner will at some point be faced with the predicament of making a change or an addition to the electric wiring schematics on board. And one often starts unscrewing cheerfully, as if standards didn't exist. But this could become life-threateningly dangerous! Work on the 110/220-volt circuit should only be performed by professionals. Improper cabling in the 12-volt circuit could also lead to damage to the yacht. Electrolysis destroys metal components on board (the engine for example) and a short circuit could even cause the entire yacht to burn down.

The literature about on-board electric wiring is extensive, but understanding and adhering to the basics of color codes for electric wiring is a good start.

Tip

Specific colors are used for the control wires for the motor and for connecting other units such as the auto-pilot, anemometer, etc. Often, these wires are also numbered. This system of coding and numbering should be clear in the yacht's wiring diagram or a diagram for a specific electronic component. In Germany, with 220-Volt and three-phase systems, the colors black and brown are principally used for live wires (as live is

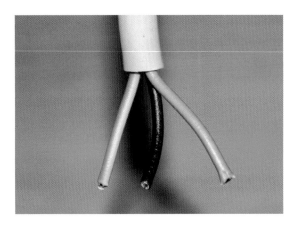

Wires will spark when the wrong colors come together.

meant any wire which lights up the live-tester). Blue is reserved for the negative, and yellow-green wire identifies the earth.

In 12- or 24-volt systems, the color red indicates positive wires and blue indicates negative wires. Wires with these colors are standard for connecting all electrical consumers.

GPS: Switching On and Feeling Good

On most yachts—including most charter yachts—a permanently installed GPS device is now commonplace. But many charter skippers bring additional mobile devices on board, so that they can avoid having to search through the instruction manual of an unfamiliar device during their valuable vacation time.

One's own device offers benefits. One can already save waypoints for the respective sailing area at home. In connection with a PC, this information can even be loaded automatically, since the appropriate information with waypoint data is available on

the market on CDs or via the Internet. But be careful! The coordinates can also be wrong. An appropriate check is thus essential. But of course, the self-introduced longitudes and latitudes could also be wrong. It is therefore truly advisable to monitor the position and course of the yacht using terrestrial navigation. Only too happily do sailors trust the treacherous "truth" on the display and think themselves on the safe side, only because of the fact that they have switched on the oh-so-wonderful device.

Quite a few skippers have gotten properly "lost," and soon they have no idea exactly where they are sailing. I, myself, have also had such an experience. On the water a skipper sailing within calling distance once asked me for directions: "Excuse me, where does one go into the Harbor in Corfu?"

These days GPS technology is part of standard equipment on every yacht.

We were practically right in front of the entrance, but he had no idea. Obviously, he had completely concentrated on the GPS device and thus neglected to look around the area. Even so, a GPS device simplifies navigation enormously, as long as one doesn't rely on it completely. Also, don't be afraid of the unfamiliar devices on board! In most cases, they already show the longitude and latitude directly after having been switched on. If you transfer this to the chart, then you instantly have your true position and can plot a course from there (don't forget the correction factors here, these are usually indicated somewhere on the chart edge).

Those who truly want to study the instruction manual can then also program waypoints and routes with the GPS. But I personally prefer to look around rather than stare at the device's miniature display. After all, I spend the whole year sitting in front of a screen.

GPS: Reception Below Deck

These days it is hard to find a yacht without a GPS receiver. On most yachts, there is even a plotter or sometimes an on-board computer, usually a laptop, which is connected with an external GPS device and navigation software.

The GPS antenna is annoying on deck, but it has to be mounted somewhere. It's already complicated enough having to weave the relatively rigid antenna cable through the smallest crevices, behind panels and through steel stanchions. The plastic antenna itself is actually in the way in every position on deck. One often sees it screwed to the stern railing, where it is well anchored, but the crew always have

Exposed position of the GPS antenna.

to take care not to sit on it accidentally or that a line doesn't get caught around the housing and simply rip the expensive item off, thus putting an end to GPS-supported navigation and a return to using good ol' sea charts and a bearing compass. So, why not install the GPS antenna in a safe location below deck?

Tip

Information signals from satellites pass through a fiberglass deck practically unhindered and can therefore also be received by the antenna below deck. You can attach it right under the cabin roof in an easily accessible area or possibly even right behind the navigation area. Attach the device cables and test the strength of the incoming signal.

In most positions, the GPS receiver will function properly below deck. The owner is spared the need to mount the cumbersome cable and antenna. Also, this location is weather proof, which means there will be no corrosion and no crew member can damage the expensive item. Another consideration is that by installing the GPS receiver below deck, the antenna cable is generally shorter, which reduces the amount of volts dropped over the line. The higher voltage input compensates for any drop in field strength the unit may experience.

This will work perfectly for GRP boats, but unfortunately isn't applicable for metal yachts.

Securing a Laptop with Bungee Cords

Ever-more computers are finding their way on board. Laptops in particular are predestined for use on yachts because of their size. But there isn't a clever mounting device available on the market that will prevent the computer from falling down. So, you may want to build one yourself. For your own yacht you can craft a stable laptop mount, but what about on a charter-yacht? You want the device to be available, but you don't want to have to disassemble and reassemble it each time you want to use it. But you also want it to be sturdy so the laptop doesn't come loose or get damaged.

Tip

A simple bungee cord can prevent the computer from slipping, especially if an anti-slip mat is placed underneath.

On most yachts you can find a ready-to-use space to set up the laptop, a space where you can also use one or two bungee cords to secure the machine from slipping or even falling.

Thanks to rubber feet, the computer is (almost) unmovable.

Always the Right Rotary Fan

A small fan, as is often happily used in cars, provides a welcome supply of fresh air on a yacht. Sometimes, however, the fan may provide too much air, or it is unbearably loud when in operation.

Now summer can come.

Tip

Electronics stores carry voltage dividers for connecting small electrical devices that need less than a 12-volt power supply. These devices reduce the 12-volt, on-board voltage to a selectable range of 1.5, 3, 4.5, 6, 7.5, or 9 volts.

The fan can be plugged in with one of these dividers. Depending on the voltage selected, the fan will run respectively slower and more smoothly.

Please note: The fan's power consumption must be smaller or at most equal to the consumption of the voltage divider. This information can be found on each product.

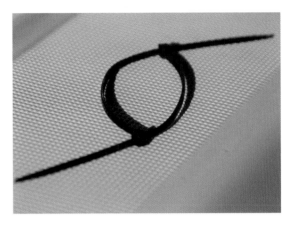

Cable ties belong in every skipper's on-board toolbox.

Extending Cable Ties and Hose Clamps

Cable ties are not only used for keeping wires neat and organized, on yachts they are used to fasten equipment securely and durably. And, if needed, they can easily be removed with a quick cut. You probably have a few cable ties on board, but sometimes the length is too short for the job at hand. They can quickly be cut shorter, but when the cable tie is too short, what then?

Tip

Simply connect two or more cable ties together to achieve the desired length.

The exact same procedure can be used on hose clamps: If one clamp is too short to fit around a thicker hose, then connect two or more until the desired length is reached.

Marine Weather on the Computer

Tip

The Hamburg, Germany,-based SEEWIS is a marine weather information system available for pleasure yachting.

This marine weather information system provides current weather information and forecasts via downloads to a personal com-

Marine weather forcasts on board? No problem with mobile access to the Internet.

puter or laptop. Hereby, the pleasure sailor can select the relevant information from a wide offering before the start of the trip and also print this out if needed.

SEEWIS covers the areas of the North and Baltic Seas, the Canadian islands, as well as the entire Mediterranean.

It is a practical tool for all skippers who use their computers on board.

Sailing with GoogleMaps

The display can be this accurate, when the images are up to date.

Tip

Google's GoogleMaps tool is also very useful for boating enthusiasts. This service is quite good because it is free and can also be used on many mobile phones in conjunction with an incorporated GPS receiver. Also, GoogleMaps, just like GoogleEarth, is immediately ready for use on practically any PC or laptop without installing any software. It only requires an Internet connection.

In addition to the known uses for GoogleEarth, street maps can also be shown and routes can be calculated and displayed. If a GPS unit is attached, then the current position can also be incorporated into the street maps and satellite images, which include street names—ideal for finding the right tavern.

The satellite images in particular offer interesting possibilities for the boating enthusiast. Here, for example, the ship's position is displayed when a GPS receiver is connected. Harbors and anchorages can be inspected with a bird's eye view. But there is one catch. Sometimes the satellite photos are not very up to date and the resolution may not be very high. It would certainly be great if the skipper could preview the area before a trip, but the maps aren't always

current, as is shown by an actual aerial image by the author. The harbor of Lakki on the Greek island Leros can be seen in the bottom right of the photo. The island lies in the eastern Aegean in the archipelago of the Dodecanese; here you can see the largest natural harbor in the Mediterranean. It is three nautical miles long. You can also see the twice-bent pier, which surrounds the inner harbor. Around the time that this image was taken, the Google image only showed a pier with a single bend, which proves that the Googleimage was a few years old.

Conclusion: Only when images are current do they provide a welcome supplement to sea charts and pilot books.

Aerial images can serve as a planning aid, but should never be used for navigation!

Proper Insulation of Power Cables

Tip

Work on a high-voltage circuit should be done by a professional! This much has to said beforehand, since working with a 110/220-volt system on board a yacht is far too dangerous for the novice. In the photo, it is easy to recognize the right way to do things and the wrong way. The cable in the left part of the image is far too thick for the job at hand. The outer insulation of the cable doesn't fit into the plug entry. The "specialist" cuts off the protecting sheath without further ado. But the sheath is there to not only protect against dirt, oil, acids, and mechanical damage, but also against excessive bending and to take up excessive tensional forces.

If the sheath is removed, then the wires bear the brunt of all of this, which cannot be good in the long run. Cracks form in the insulation, wires snap off, and eventually breakage or short circuits are the results.

The presence of sea and rainwater accelerates this process. But even the loose wires are still too thick for feeding into the

Sloppiness with the electric can be lethal!

plug and the two parts of the plug cannot be pressed firmly together. Water penetration, corrosion, and failure are the results. On the right side of the photo the correct cable incorporation looks really good! A water-insulating, shrink tubing is placed over the outer sheath of the cable, which is also an effective protection against bending. The through hole is big enough and sealed sufficiently with a rubber seal. Here water and dirt stay outside and the current stays in.

Thick power supply cables for air conditioning and refrigeration.

6. Safety and Seamanship

Slippery When Wet!

"Slippery when wet!" This warning is found worldwide, prominently displayed on countless steps and floors—just not on yachts. But this is exactly where it is known to often become wet, from sea water and/or rain. And furthermore, holding a secure stance on a slanting and rolling deck is often vitally important. But even so, many manufacturers renounce not only attaching a warning label, but also applying a practical top-layer to the deck that makes a solid stance possible. A mere corrugated gelcoat is simply not enough. On the contrary, when water remains in the small wells, the bow is turned into an ice skating rink. Retrofitting is therefore necessary and recommended.

Tip

The industry offers a wide variety of different materials. One option is a coating that is brushed on like paint. Others come as mats that have to be glued on. Finally, one could opt to lay a beautiful teak deck. The main differences among these options are price and the finishing. While one could use the paint or glue the mats quite simply oneself, the teak deck would be quite a task, even for experienced DIYers. All these surface coverings usually do their job quite well. The durability can, however, vary greatly and it may depend on which part of the yacht you are treating. Strong UV radiation, for example, can make many materials appear old very quickly. Even so, a non-slip deck covering is a bit of security. Non-slip footwear also helps a little, but only the combination of the two can provide a secure stance.

Whoever slips here could hurt themselves pretty badly.

Avoiding Drama at Port

The best captains are known to all-knowingly sit on shore. The most aggressive captains sit on neighboring yachts and fear for their valuable vessels. But what happens when a more or less well-planned harbor maneuver goes totally wrong? Or even better, how can one prevent a harbor maneuver from going so wrong that it leads to damage?

Tip

Here, preparation is half the battle. Those who plan to sail into a harbor, should have studied the pilot guide beforehand to know where the moorings are, how big the area of maneuverability is, as well as the depth at hand.
One should know whether moorings are at hand, if one's own anchor is to be used, if one needs to moor alongside, rafting, and so on. Before entering the harbor, fenders should be attached in positions appropriate for the

planned maneuver, and lines, boat hooks, anchors, etc. rigged to run clear. Knowing the wind direction is crucial for the maneuver since a breeze from the wrong direction can quickly push a yacht astray. The skipper discusses the maneuver with his/her crew, shows them their positions, and explains what each one's task is. He should also have a plan B in mind. Now, the skipper and crew can arrive in a relaxed mood, enjoy the scenery, and take their vacation photos. A *marinero*, or "pilot," often points out the berth when coming in. In many harbors one can even reserve a berth via telephone, Internet, or VHF radio. Also, open berths sometimes have a "green" plaque. The skipper now starts the mooring maneuver and carefully moves the yacht towards the mooring.

Here comes the most important point! When he notices that the maneuver is starting to get out of control, there should be an immediate: "Abort, sailing out and start again!" A new try is far smarter than trying to save a maneuver gone wrong through force— that won't work anymore. As a result, the yacht will lie skew and unable to maneuver in between neighboring yachts. Here, steel grates on fiberglass, anchors bore into woodwork, and, through courageous attempts at holding off, stanchions are bent, kinked, and finally snapped off. Bow pulpits are bent and beautiful finishes scratched.

The crews of the vessels involved work with joined forces in order to free the disabled yacht.

Their skippers pull at their hair because of the damage to their yachts, while the crew of the incident-causing yacht stares into the void relatively apathetically, unable to be of any real help. That is real life harbor drama! But with a little preparation and practice handling the yacht, the maneuver would have gone off smoothly and perhaps even elegantly; and the best captains, namely those sitting on land, would have had nothing to complain about.

Mooring maneuver: Skipper and crew in stress, a common sight in the marina.

Renouncing Sunscreen

For many vacationers, a sailing trip in the South is an opportunity to arm themselves with bottles and tubes of product for basking in the sun on deck. This is part of the planned relaxation. But part of the plan should also involve men and women lying on large towels, to prevent the applied sunscreen from ending up on the deck surface, since this could have catastrophic results. All these oily sun creams can easily get smeared on deck, creating a surface as slippery as an ice rink. The author himself has already had two slippery encounters of this kind as he enthusiastically marched on deck while doing work and slipped on the oily film. The first time he tore a ligament in his foot and the second time he fell with one leg into an open hatch, his ribs colliding with the vertically opened hatch cover.

Tip

Therefore: No oily sunscreens or oil on board! There are sun-creams and other protective fluids which are quickly absorbed into the skin that don't leave any greasy residue.

In particular, when grease or oil mixes with water and sea salt, the result is an emul-

Is there anything better than lying in the sun all oiled up and enjoying your free time? But be careful! When suntan oil or greasy cream ends up on deck, it can become dangerously slippery.

sion that is as slippery as liquid soap. With this substance on deck, a "slip with serious results" is likely in the cards.

Another tip for sun worshipers: You can also tan in the shade. It is far healthier for the skin and you hardly need any sun protection. And anyway, those who bake in the sun for ten hours with 20 proof sun protection receive the same amount of sun as one who lies in the sun for half an hour without sun screen. A light shirt and hat are effective ways to avoid sunburn the rest of the time.

Uncluttered Lines in the Aft Locker

Many yachts have something in common: the stern lockers are unfathomably large and deep, and the items stored in them can only be regained once this tomb has been completely emptied. Plastic crates and other stackable containers have proven effective at managing this space. But chaos often breaks out on board when a specific line that is urgently needed must be retrieved from the depths of the stern locker.

But this FUBAR situation with the lines is easy to avoid.

Tip

Screw small and affordable cleats onto the inner wall of the stern locker, vertically oriented. Then take a line that is about 3.25' (1 m) long, tie the ends together, and form a loop. Now pass the thin loop through the bight of the coiled line and then simply hook it onto the cleat.

The result: All lines hang on the wall of the stern-locker neatly and ready for use and can be removed at any time without getting tangled.

Swimming Off the Yacht

On trips to warm sailing areas, a swim off the yacht is an integral part of enjoying your holiday. Jumping into the cool water of the open ocean far from the coast is an exceptional experience. Here you can truly experience the vastness of the ocean.

But a few safety precautions should also be taken to prevent the fun from turning into a serious situation. Yachts have often been found adrift, showing no signs of damage, but with no trace of the crew. It is highly

This looks neat and well organized.

A swim in the sea is refreshing and can be enjoyed without worry, once preparations for getting back on board have been made.

likely that the crew went for a swim without leaving a crew member on board or letting the swimming ladder down. The yacht's hull was too high for the swimmers to climb back up.

Tip
Only undertake such an action in calm seas and away from sailing areas or other shipping lanes. Carefully secure the sails that have been taken down, because even a small breeze can cause the yacht to move and then the swimmers will have a difficult time catching up.

One crew member who is competent handling the engine should always remain on board. And the swimming ladder should always be let down into the water. Only then can the swimming fun begin.

It is also popular to cast a swimming line, attached to the deck, into the water. Swimmers can use this to be towed behind the moving yacht. But be careful of the propeller! Your legs as well as the line could get caught in it.

Lanyard at the Helm Position

On every yacht or boat there is always something that needs to be lashed down. You will need a variety of lanyards for this: short and thin, thicker, stronger, longer, or sometimes even a sail tie or a bungee cord.

Tip
All these pieces of line can, of course, be stored in a locker, but then you always have to go in search of the right one. It is

There is always use for a lanyard.

A few years ago, the species was accidentally released into the Mediterranean by the Aquarium of Monaco, and since then it has been spread incisively by clinging to the anchor gear of yachts, among other things. Even in the remote anchorages of Greece, off the Turkish coast, the algae grows over the bottom and overwhelms everything else. Since it is not endemic to the Mediterranean, it is not consumed by fish or other sealife and grows unabated.

Tip

Yachties can actively help avoid further spreading Caulerpa Taxifolia. Each time you raise the anchor and chain, you should check that leaves or shoots haven't entangled themselves in the gear. Otherwise you will be carrying the plant to your next anchorage.

very practical if this collection of line has a home somewhere nearby the helm pedestal. If they are all neatly organized here, at a glance one can see the length and strength of each line and immediately judge which one is needed in each case.

The "Killer Algae" Caulerpa Taxifolia

Caulerpa Taxifolia is a type of algae that is very popular for use in seawater aquariums, because it looks pretty when the fish swim through the leaf blades. To marine biologists, however, Caulerpa Taxifolia is simply known as the "killer algae," because of how quickly this water plant has spread throughout the Mediterranean region.

The "killer algae" is spreading through the Mediterranean at an alarming rate.

The Endless Jibe Preventer

The endless jibe preventer is one sure method of keeping the mainsail in check. Who likes to make trips to the bow in rough weather to secure the "preventer" to the bow cleat, getting drenched along the way? Not to mention the danger of having a sailor on the bow! The sensible alternative is the "endless jibe preventer," which I have been able to use on all the yachts I have sailed.

The endless jibe preventer keeps the mainsail in check.

Tip
Approximately two boat-lengths of strong line without knots is needed for setting up this preventer. Start with one end, which is, as usual, tied to the end of the boom. The free end is led to the bow outside of the shrouds where it isn't secured, but merely led through. The line is also led through the second bow cleat (if available). On the other side pass the line once more to the end of the boom outside of the shrouds. This end is also attached there. A simple block in the bow area can also be elegantly rigged for leading the endless jibe preventer back.
Now the "preventer" can be hauled tight from the cockpit on each respective tack and secured to a stern cleat, for example. Now nobody needs to scramble about on the foredeck. For a jibe, release the endless preventer and perform the maneuver as usual, the preventer is tightened on the new tack.

When the Snorkeler Becomes the Tow Boat

Has this ever happened to you? No matter how well-prepared you are for casting off in the marina, this still happens. The yacht lies across the other vessels, their anchor chains/lines end up between the rudder and the keel and then you are left unable to maneuver. Does it sound familiar? And what did you do to get out of this situation? Naturally, you do everything you can to keep the yacht off the other vessel's stern or bow pulpits. In light winds this isn't such a big problem. The real problem is that the chains and lines hanging around make it impossible to use the motor.

Flippers, mask, and snorkel should be ready for use because you may have to act as a bow tower in certain situations.

Three Left, Three Right, Don't Drop Any

When using "Mediterranean mooring" (i.e., lying on the bow anchor with the stern lines to the pier), it is always interesting to see where, when, and how the fenders are attached.

Some avoid these rubber sausages completely, either in order to prevent the yacht from getting dirty or to avoid diminishing its aesthetic value. Without these protective items, however, the result can be ugly scratches on the sides of the hull. Others attach one or two fenders amidships and consider themselves well protected. And some skippers will have a crew member positioned on the coach roof with a roaming fender. But, as is often the case, there is an easier way.

Tip

One practical solution is to lower the tender and outboard to the water, tie a towing line to the middle of the yacht—to the chain plates, for example—and tow the yacht out of its precarious situation.

But usually quick action is required and this excludes protracted handling. This means putting on the flippers and jumping in the water. It only takes seconds. Now the "rescuer" swims to midship, somewhere around the level of the shrouds, and inch-by-inch pushes the yacht out of the dangerous situation. This does require some powerful water treading, but the flippers will help.

Tip

▶ When mooring in reverse, the stern is, of course, the part which will come into contact with the neighboring yachts first. Thus, the first and most important fender should be placed here. This, as well as the rest of the rubber protectors, should be attached from their top right below the deck height on most yachts.

▶ Amidships is the widest point and when moving in there will thus arise various points of contact here. Ergo: there should also be a fender here.

▶ The foreship area also needs a fender since a side wind can easily push the bow to leeward during the mooring maneuver, thus requiring effective protection.

▶ Further available rubber buffers increase the effective protection, the fact that fenders need to be attached to both sides is obvious.

With proper fender positioning one can avoid nasty collisions when mooring and save one crew member from the thankless job of managing the "roaming fender."

▶ Finally, there should also be a fender on the stern, so that even if the gear shift mechanism gets stuck, no serious damage will occur.

If the mooring was successful and the yacht is secure, then the skipper can adjust the position and height of the fenders with regards to the neighboring vessels. If the anchor, lines, and fenders are prepared beforehand, then the crew won't be in a rush during the maneuver and there can even be time for some photos during entry into the harbor. Obviously, the rubber devices should remain on the sides for security when casting-off.

Thus, the "roaming fender" has become obsolete and an additional crew member can actively participate in handling the stern lines.

One Step, One Turn, the Hatch is Open

This tip isn't meant to be used for intrusion, but here is a trick for getting into the yacht when the rest of the crew, along with the yacht key, have disappeared among the harbor bars. At the same time, it also goes to show how easy it is for thieves to break into a yacht's interior.

Tip
Have you ever tried to open or close a deck hatch from the deck, using the grips on the outside of the cover? With a new hatch with a fully intact rubber seal, it is fairly difficult. But if one places one's body-weight on it by standing on the edge of the hatch-cover, the seal is compressed and the deck-hatch can be opened or closed easily.

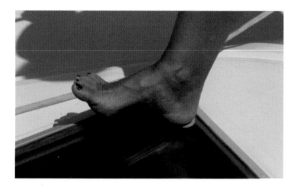

Luckily not all thieves know this trick yet.

The practical and multiple uses of the bicycle spanner wrench are often overlooked on the yacht.

But what if the hatch that needs to be opened has no outer grip? The trick works in almost the exact same way: Stand with your heel directly on the outer "opposing knob" of the inner locking handle.

If you make a strong turn with your foot to the left or right—as you may have learned if you took dance lessons—the hatch handle turns with and the hatch can be opened. Of course, this doesn't work with hatches that have a locking device on the inside.

Incidentally: In some areas of the world, charterers who wish to find their valuables safe after returning from a trip to land should try this trick before leaving their yacht.

The Bicycle Spanner Wrench as a Multi-Purpose Tool

Tip
There is a specific multi-use tool found in the toolbox of many cyclists: the bicycle spanner wrench. This tool fits nuts of various standard sizes, which are ideal for many different uses on board. But the real benefit is that you don't have to carry an entire set of heavy wrenches on board.

On smaller yachts in particular, the weight of equipment and outfitting plays an important role with regards to yacht trim and speed. The bicycle spanner wrench helps reduce weight while providing many tools.

Paint Tray Recycling

Every amateur painter knows and hates the fact that every painting job is followed by the need to tediously clean equipment. This is a time-consuming job that certainly extends the life of your tools, but it usually generates a bit of a mess. The following idea shows that there is another way.

Tip
This tip is courtesy of a Turkish shipyard worker who painted the bottom of my yacht armed with a roller, painting trays, and a few buckets of anti-fouling agent.

Before he poured the anti-fouling agent into the painting tray, he placed the tray into a large plastic bag. Only then did he carefully pour the paint into the paint tray. He then soaked the paint roller as usual. After he completed the paint job he pulled the plastic bag from the walls of the tray and threw it in the garbage. The paint tray was free of

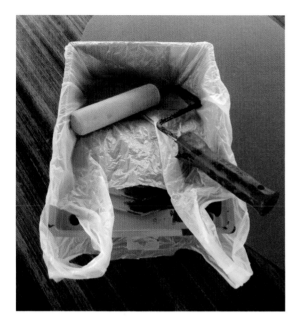

Simply place the painting tools in a plastic bag—which eliminates the need to clean up afterwards.

stains and didn't need to be cleaned—I still use the same one today.

Repairing Broken Pipes and Hoses

Usually the worst equipment malfunctions happen at the worst moments, when you are far away from any hardware stores. Perhaps a hose burst or a metal pipe rusted through and started to leak. Good advice is expensive here, but the yacht could go down.

Tip

Let's do what doctors would: A broken leg is encased in a plaster bandage and all is well again. Of course plaster isn't an appropriate material for use on board or on the engine. Because of the vibrations and movement of the yacht, a brittle plaster cast would quickly be destroyed. But a bandage can be used if it is impregnated with the right material. The well-known sealant Sikaflex combined with a bandage is perfect for creating a durable, yet flexible, sealing bandage. Sikaflex sticks to various surfaces and the bandage provides the necessary base. This method can even be used to make an emergency repair of the exhaust hose, if it has become porous with age and exhaust gases mixed with cooling water end up inside the yacht. Usually, the mixture of exhaust gas and water does not have a temperature and there is no danger of combustion. If the temperatures are higher, then a fiberglass mat can also be used as a base. Here, the appropriate binding substance would be epoxy or, if it becomes even hotter, liquid metal would come into play. After curing, both of the latter materials can even be filed, flexed, or drilled, seeing as they become truly hard. There is even a special epoxy that can cure under water.

And in the case of damage, it is certainly worth it to try placing an underwater epoxy bandage over the affected area.

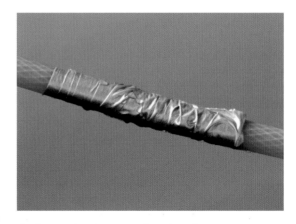

An improvisation can often last for years.

Dangerous Debris at Sea

In pleasant weather, light winds, and good visibility, sighting a steel pantry that has been cast overboard by a large vessel in the middle of the Adriatic is not too alarming. The object can be easily spotted by the lookout from afar and even with an engaged autopilot it can be avoided effortlessly. But what if this solid chunk shows up at night? It might be too late to deviate course and a large crash will summon the crew on deck when the yacht collides with the floating debris. A solidly constructed yacht should actually be able to withstand such a hit and the damage should be limited to a few, although deep, scratches and dents. But if the floating debris is more solid than the bow or hull, things can quickly become critical.

Flotsam can create bad leaks.

Tip

This is no place for a general statement on the actions to be taken in case of a collision with floating debris. Whole essays have already been written on the subject, as can be found on the Internet. According to popular opinion, such a collision doesn't necessarily involve only the bow area. In many articles it is clear that damage can also occur to the rudder system. Therefore, the skipper should not only be mentally prepared for pumping out seawater and sealing holes, but also for rigging an emergency rudder.

Prevention is important at all times! The lookout walk is by no means an unpleasant duty, and helps prevent calamities. A radar device might display the metal chest on the screen, but sometimes flotsam can be material that is not radar reflective or a swell may disguise the echoes of such small objects.

There are also specialized, forward orientated, sonar devices and outrageously expensive infrared cameras that can be sometimes used on super yachts in order to avoid collisions with floating debris. But unfortunately, even the best lookout cannot spot all of the abundant, flat-on-the-water objects drifting about, and at night not at all. Those who sail at night should stay out of shipping routes to take advantage of the chance that any objects which may have gone overboard from large vessels will have divided up by the time they reach areas of less sea traffic. Of course, a bit of luck is also involved.

The fact that a bay is well protected can be determined from afar and not only by the large amount of yachts lying at anchor.

Recognizing Sheltered Coastlines

While there are some sheltered coastal areas in the Mediterranean, others are unprotected from wind and waves. Here are some tips on how they can easily be distinguished.

Tip

If the plant life on the coast grows up close to the waterline, then even in bad weather the waves don't get very high. This means that high waves don't develop in front of the shore. But if the rocks on the shore are bare and jagged, this means that the waves can reach the shore unhindered and that the spray in certain places can reach a height of more than 30 feet. The result is that all the plant life dies and only the bare rocks remain. In this way, the boating enthusiast can determine whether a shore offers shelter or not from a long distance away.

Using a Bungee Cord as a Shock Absorber

Especially when a yacht is going to spend a long time in a berth, every owner makes sure that it is well secured. This means that mooring lines and springs keep the yacht in the desired position. Here the lines should neither be too long, in which case the yacht will have too much "play" in the berth, nor should they be too taut, since that would put a lot of strain on the fittings and lines. In both cases, the fittings, in this case the cleats, take a lot of stress during the tugging. The force generated when a heavy yacht rump is pushed by a swell, pulling on the lines could strain the cleats and rip them out of the hull.

Bungee-cords take pressure off the fittings.

Tip

Owners can use various aids to rig so-called shock absorbers. It brakes the hard tugging and conserves the fittings. Thanks to their extreme flexibility, solid rubber straps are perfect additions to the mooring lines.

Thus, the shorter lines keep the yacht well in its berth, but in case of swell, the mooring lines can stretch and thereby effectively dampen the yacht's movements.

Hoist Markings on the Hull

Every year a situation arises that makes the yacht owner's heart beat faster. Cranes are

With the help of decals, it is easier for the crane operator to find the right positions for the straps.

a must! And every time the crane comes out there are horrific scenes going through his/ her mind. The yacht could slide out of the straps and crash to the ground, or the straps might be attached to the wrong positions and press the sail drive to the inside. Here the shaft can also be bent, or, or, or...!

Tip

Here is a simple trick to regain your peace of mind. Attach decals to both sides of the hull, underneath the toe-rail for example, that thus indicate the correct and safe positions for the crane straps to the crane operator.

Long Release Cord for Snap Shackle

Snap shackles are used not only on sailing yachts, but on motor yachts as well. They are practical, thus easy to open and close. Usually, there is a small loop attached to the release bolt so that the shackle can be opened easily by tugging on the line.

This is completely good enough for most applications. But sometimes you may need to provide the snap shackle with a remote release. This can be useful on the clew of the spinnaker or on any line that is used to lower the tender from the deck to the water. Thus, it is no longer necessary to climb into the dingy in order to release the snap shackle and thereby the line.

Tip

And this is how you proceed. Tie the long rip line to the release bolt. Attach the other end to the halyard or davit line of the same length, with a clove hitch for example, so that the help line doesn't swing around loosely. In this way, it is always ready.

A release cord for the snap shackle saves climbing trips.

Lines in the Propeller...and Down You Go

On some occasions a line, fishing line, or even a fishing net will get caught in the propeller. The crew may be cruising along merrily or busy with a mooring maneuver when suddenly, the engine simply stops without warning.

After the first few seconds of shock, the skipper will disengage the drive and try a start attempt. No problem! The diesel immediately springs back to life. But with the next attempt to engage, it stalls again. The situation is now slowly becoming clear. The propeller is jammed and the yacht is drifting

on the water unable to maneuver. If there is enough wind, then sail power can be used to sail into the next harbor or sheltered bay, in order to free the propeller. But if it is calm and there is little or no swell, then immediate remedy is feasible, since the yacht hull is lying calmly in the water.

But if the mishap occurs during maneuvering in a tight bay or right in the harbor entrance, then quick anchoring could save one from going aground or colliding with other yachts. And now comes the question: What do you do?

Tip

Tediously poking around with the boat hook from the swimming ladder or the tender usually doesn't work. The quickest way is to remove the foreign material while snorkeling, using flippers, snorkel, and diving mask, which should always be on board. The advantages are that the diver can see exactly where it is caught and can even—at least partially—work with both hands. Thicker lines which have only been wound around the propeller or shaft a few times can mostly be removed without tools by

Each crew member should be have some snorkeling skills—for example, to clear the propeller.

turning the disengaged propeller. Nylon lines or even nets can pull themselves really tight, they can even get melted from stretching. The only thing that helps here is tough untangling, wind by wind, using a big knife or screwdriver. You can also cut through the using a hacksaw.

In extremely tough cases, for example in the case of a sail drive line that has gone into the unreachable gap behind the propeller directly onto the shaft, then the quickest way to do the repair is to dismount the entire propeller and comfortably untangle it on deck, re-mounting it afterwards. That is, if the propeller isn't baked on!

Once the propeller has been freed, the sail can continue.

In particularly serious cases the shaft could be bent by the force of the tangle. One should pay attention to this, listening for new and unfamiliar noises while motoring.

Of course, the engine has to be switched off during any of these operations! With a running motor there is a considerable risk for injury.

A Tarp as a Fender Guard

On board, one could say that fenders represent our "bodily-contact" with the outside world. They prevent the fragile hull from coming in contact with the sharp-edged marina wall. In swell, it rolls between the hull sides and the wall and dampens the movement. But here it also takes up the dirt clinging to the wall together with grit and transfers these to the side of the hull. This not only results in unsightly stains, but sometimes the grit also scratches the delicate gelcoat or the paint work.

Using a tarp as a fender shield protects the hull side.

Tip

A tarp placed between the hull and the fender prevents dirt from transferring to the hull. For this purpose, a solid piece of material is provided with grommet holes on one side so that it can be attached to the railing. Although the fender still becomes dirty, the side of the hull now remains clean. Wash the tarp from time to time. If you placed the tarp between the wall and the fender, then it would quickly be destroyed by the sharp edges of the harbor wall.

Testing the Quality of the Engine Oil

Tip

There is a simple trick for getting an idea of how good or poor the quality of the oil in the engine is. Place a piece of kitchen towel, toilet paper, blotting paper, or even a coffee filter on the table. Let a drop of oil from the

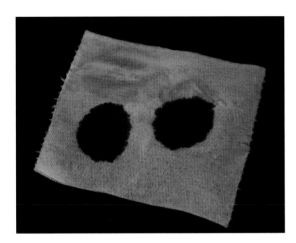

Regular oil tests extend the life of the engine.

only identical life vests available.

But when things get serious out at sea, nobody knows which vest is his/her own.

Tip

I have solved this problem in a humorous way. All my life vests have been named after famous pirates. Thus, each crew member simply remembers the respective buccaneer's name (e.g., Sir Francis Drake, Captain Blackbeard, or even Klaus Störtebeker) and in this way the life vests have been effectively assigned. This measure moreover contributes to the entertainment of the trip, since the meaningful names provide much potential for fun and jesting.

dipstick drip on the paper. After a while the oil drop will be absorbed and a round stain can be observed.

If the stain is light brown, then the oil is fresh, if it is black and several circles have formed around the center, then the oil is old and full of impurities. In the first case all is well, in the second an oil change is advisable in the near future.

The oil can also be tested by rubbing a drop between the thumb and forefinger: If it feels rough and not slippery at all, then the lubrication effect has completely abated. When you can truly feel the residue particles contained in the oil, the oil is spent and should be changed.

Providing the Life Vests with Names

Many skippers have experienced the same thing: a new crew member arrives on board, the skipper gives an extensive safety briefing, and of course the life vests are tried on and adjusted to the size of each new crew member. As on many other ships, there are

When the life vests have been provided with names, there is no danger of mixing up the gear in a dangerous situation.

Concave Helmsman's Seat

Especially on longer passages, the helmsman cannot stand continuously, he wants to sit down while performing his/her duty. But in most cases cockpits don't offer any especially comfortable sitting positions—and none at all while heeling.

Tip
For this reason many ships have a special helmsman's seat built in. It is concave and provides a comfortable seat in any degree of heel. Slipping is impossible because of the curvature so that the helmsman can perform his/her job well—and be securely supported.

Sometimes one finds a seat which is curved in a round form. It might look a bit more attractive, but it doesn't provide such a comfortable or secure seat. This version is still better than a completely flat one, from which one continually slips when one leans to the side during heeling in a seaway.

The helmsman can sit upright on any degree of heel.

Mousing the Shackles Using Cable Ties

Not every sailor trusts that a well-tightened shackle won't undo itself. A shackle can be secured using different materials.

Tip
Wire is a suitable material for this purpose, for example. Wire either doesn't rust, but is hard to bend, or it bends easily but rusts quickly. One can also secure a shackle using whipping twine. It just takes time to do the winding. Mousing a shackle goes very quickly and is very secure when using a cable tie from the hardware store. It is threaded through the eye of the shackle

Non-detachable bolt.

bolt and pulled tight around the body of the shackle. A cut from a knife is all that is needed to free it.

Snorkeling and Scuba Diving for Working Under Water

Confident with a wet suit and diving tank.

Sometimes a problem arises under water. A line ends up in the propeller, a seacock gets clogged, or an anchor gets stuck. Before one has the yacht hoisted out for a lot of money or just leaves it drifting on the surface unable to maneuver, one can take care of things oneself under water.

Tip
Every skipper should be able to snorkel a little bit at least. The fascinating underwater world alone makes it worth going exploring with the diving mask from time to time. Basic equipment, consisting of a well-fitting diving mask, a snorkel, and a pair of flippers should have their place on every yacht. In cold water or locations with intense sun radiation, like the tropics, an old T-shirt can help a little against the cold and/or to prevent sunburn. The best protection is, of course, a proper neoprene wet suit. But then you also have to wear a weight belt so you don't float around on the water surface like a cork.
If you need to dive down to the propeller, you first have to get your breathing under control. The more relaxed the body is, the longer you can last under water with the held-in air. This is easier said than done when the yacht is drifting towards land unable to maneuver and panic reigns on board. Even so, without calm, snorkeling doesn't work and ear- or head-aches due to wrongful breathing could be the relatively unpleasant results.

Before diving, breathe in and out deeply three or four times through the snorkel and then go under. If you are only diving one or two meters, there shouldn't be any pressure equalization needed, but when you feel pressure on your ears (they should never hurt!), you should squeeze your nose using thumb and index finger through the gap in the mask and "sneeze." The ears will quickly pop, relieving the pressure.
After diving, purge the snorkel with a strong blow and start the cycle again.
As soon as everything is in order again and the diving session has ended, a warm shower, warm drink, warm clothing, and a little rest is recommended.

Sponge on a Long Leash

Sometimes it is really annoying that certain areas on board are seemingly unreachable by hand. Either the inspection holes are too small or the bilge is so far down that one cannot reach it by hand. No matter how much you contort yourself, you just cannot reach.

Not all holes are man sized.

And it is exactly in these unreachable areas that condensation usually likes to form little pools. The little puddles can't remain there forever, but how do you get rid of them?

Tip
A small sponge attached to a string or stick can get to the most hard-to-reach corners. In this way, the water can be removed easily without acrobatic feats.

Floating Lines on Fishing Buoys

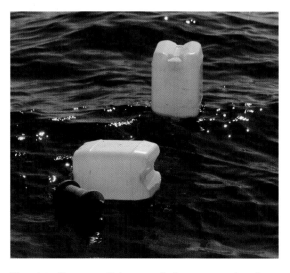

Floating lines on fisherman's buoys can be dangerous.

We have hardly left the narrow harbor and already we can feel the vastness of the ocean.... And it is easy to forget that there are certain "nautical obstacles" right beside us. Here I don't mean continents, islands, other ships, or navigation aids, but fisherman's nets, lobster pots, and in particular their markers. Especially in the southern regions and beyond the Mediterranean, fisherman use any possible floating object to mark their nets, long lines, and lobster pots. This includes used plastic containers and bottles of all colors and Styrofoam packaging—just about anything that floats.

It doesn't have to be big, just large enough to be able to keep the line which it has attached to it on the surface. The fisherman knows exactly where he has set his/ her trapping devices—the yachtie does not. For us sailors, this means that also on the open ocean, mostly close to the coast, we have to keep a lookout for these floating objects and keep a wide berth when passing them, since the fisherman often include another small snare in the form of a floating line. A buoyant line is attached to the buoy, leading into the depths to the net. Because this line is mostly longer than the depth, an amount of line is usually floating virtually invisible on the surface—and this to windward of the buoy!

If one now passes close to windward of the buoy in such a case, then the line will get caught on the keel, rudder, or propeller and the yacht will be left unable to maneuver. One can imagine what would happen if this situation took place in strong winds. Use of the engine is prevented by the line in the prop. The yacht together with the net drifts in the middle of nowhere, and if a volunteer jumps into the water armed with diving mask and knife, he would find himself in real danger, if the strong winds do not exclude this action completely.

Tip

As a rule, pass these "buoys" in the lee, and one shouldn't have any problems.

companies also perform a safety briefing and may even complete a rescue drill. This should also take place on a yacht.

The mere fact of having life vests on board does not suffice. Anyone who has ever tried to put on a life vest over oil skins on a rolling ship while also having to adjust it to size, knows what I mean. This is why, even on a sunny trip in the Mediterranean, there should be a fitting of the life vests with adjustment made for individual body size. Those crew members, who have to go onto the foredeck in bad weather, should also try on and adjust their safety harnesses. Only then can it been assured that this safety equipment can be reliably used in heavy weather and on a rolling ship with the looming threat of seasickness. The following information should also be included in the safety briefing: Location and functionality of the fire extinguishers, handling the life raft, use of the life ring, conduct in man-overboard situations, and making emergency calls on the VHF. Only then will the crew act correctly in emergency situations and the skipper can be exempted from liability through negligence.

Safety on Board

Many trips are made by thrown-together crews. Often, there are beginners on board who aren't familiar with the handling of a yacht or on-board conduct. It is the task of the skipper to form a seaworthy crew out of a group of people who are interested in sailing. First and foremost, this concerns safety.

Tip

It is essential to have a safety briefing with all crew members before the trip, while still in the harbor. Also, for the sake of possible liability issues in case an accident or mishap should occur, airlines and ocean-liner

Golden rule on board: No casting off without a safety briefing.

Whipping as Gelcoat Protector

Tip

On many yachts, a simple wooden plank or a modified aluminum ladder from the hardware store is used instead of a true gangway. In order to prevent this gangway, which rests on deck, from scratching the delicate gelcoat, I have placed a whipping on mine. It is tied on in the same way as on a line, with the difference that a 0.5" (12 mm) line is used instead of the thin whipping twine—this could also be an old off-cut out of the stern locker.

Without whipping it would rub quite a bit.

Toilet Care

The on-board toilet is surely one of the most-used accessories on a yacht. Intensive care and maintenance are essential for problem-free use. Unfortunately, these are some of the least favorite activities on board.

Good maintenance assures a long life span.

"I'd rather be up to the elbows in used oil, than repair the toilet," is something many skippers say. But the regular disassembly and maintenance of the on-board toilet isn't nearly as unpleasant as the forced repair at sea, when it is truly clogged.

Tip

As is the case with dental hygiene, prevention is better than repair. Thus, the pump interior and hoses can be freed of urine deposits using a simple coffee machine descaler. The substance is poured into the toilet bowl and taken up into the system with a few pump strokes. Leave it in to take effect and do its work. Simple vinegar from the supermarket also helps.

In order to keep the sensitive rubber valves nice and supple, simply pour a little bit of oil into the bowl and pump it through. Vegetable oil isn't suitable for this purpose since it has the property of hydrolyzing when combined with water. One ends up with a greasy mass and resinous calcium soap in the toilet which blocks the pump. Simple baby or motor oil lubricates the toilet pump for a long time.

There is also a special toilet oil on the market that has the same effect. All these oils are poured into the toilet bowl and are then introduced through a few pump strokes. The time between maintenance checks as well as the life span of the toilet pump can be considerably lengthened in this way.

Funnel as Rat Deterrent

In many marinas one isn't safe from small and unwelcome guests. Rats are found all around the world. I like to call them "long-tailed hamsters" for the sake of jumpy co-sailors. But it's no fun when these small rodents slip on board at night and gnaw at anything edible. Since they are now also going for hoses and electric cables, they are no longer just a nuisance, but dangerous. Usually, they have left the ship by morning, but not without leaving the evidence of their presence behind.

Tip

The skipper has to come up with some way of preventing them from climbing on board in the first place. And the measure is only truly effective when all connections to land have been made rat-proof. This means that the gangway should hover at least half a meter above the harbor wall. The best is to simply bring it on deck.

The small animals like to travel to the yacht across the mooring lines. A large plastic funnel simply slid over the lines effectively deters the rodent's onslaught.

Round metal plates are also often used. One can easily make them from the lid of a paint can by punching a hole in the middle and

A plastic funnel slid over the lines effectively keeps the rats on land.

cutting a slit for slipping it on. And while we are on the subject of protecting ourselves, long-tailed hamsters can swim very well! So be sure to secure the anchor chain in the same way as the mooring lines.

Cover for the Lines

All lines on board of a yacht wear more or less quickly. They are stressed in blocks and squashed on cleats, but it's the mooring lines that have to endure the most. On land, they are secured around rusty bollards, sharp-edged rings, and raw concrete, so that it doesn't take long for them to become not only unsightly with dirt, but also to chafe and finally snap.

Ropework is too expensive not to be protected.

Animal love or fear of water?

Tip

Many yacht sailors use hoses that are slipped over the lines and, for example, placed around the bollard.

An easier way is to cut a hose of at least 20" (50 cm) into a spiral form. The crew can also put line protector on this afterwards. Thus, one moors as usual, without having to worry about additional components. Place the preventers over the mooring lines at the end of the mooring maneuver.

Keeping the Dog Afloat

Every dog can swim by nature, but even a four-legged animal has difficulties keeping its head above water in heavy swell. And anyone who has seen how quickly a dog loses it's orientation under water and starts to panic knows how important it is to have one's dog wear a life vest on board.

Tip

Life vests for dogs are thus by no means a novel, snobbish accessory for crazy dog fanatics. Of course, dogs don't need as large a flotation component as a non-swim-mer would to survive in the water, but the life vest is the right aid for getting one's beloved pet quickly and safely back on board.

Since there is a strong grab handle on the top of the vest, you can use a boat hook to fish for the dog and pull the animal back on board. Smaller dogs can then be pulled quickly and safely from the water.

The dog's life vest is also a practical companion when disembarking with the tender. Without it, you either have to try balancing the loved one on your arm or pull it over the thin gangplank by force, which comes close to strangulation and isn't popular with the animals at all.

Petroleum Jelly is No Wonder Cure

Lubricating, greasing, oiling, making things move again—these are all recurring tasks on board. The owner has a seemingly endless choice of sprays, tubes, and bottles of product at his/her disposal.

Both marine outfitters and home hardware stores have a variety of products available with very specific purposes.

He who greases well, sails well.

The skipper is spoiled for choice. Usually you wouldn't want to tie up a whole locker just for housing these various lubrications, so you have to look for products that can be used universally or which at least have a wide range of applications.

Tip

Petroleum jelly is one such multi-purpose substance. It has excellent lubrication properties, has a transparent color, it keeps on lubricating for a long time, and it's cheap. With it zips, blocks, traveler tracks, and many other things slide as if they were greased. Petroleum jelly is ideal for greasing and protecting items on board. With the substance, cans and even eggs can last longer. Smear petroleum jelly on cans so they don't start to rust and eggs will stay fresh for a long time!

But there's one thing you shouldn't do: petroleum jelly doesn't belong on rubber components! If these two materials come into contact, the rubber becomes weak and wavy, even porous. This includes the dinghy's air valves, diving suits and their zips, as well as other rubber and latex products. Petroleum jelly is available at the grocery store, hardware store, and the pharmacy. The small tubes are practical and affordable.

The More the Better

Tip

The bathroom shouldn't have a bad smell! If you flush generously after your "business" has been done, then there shouldn't be any bad odors.

The on-board practice should be that roughly 15 to 20 pumps are sufficient to flush the toilet bowl, toilet pump, and the subsequent waste pipe clear with clean water.

If any residue remains in the pump or the pipe, then an unpleasant smell will build

Sufficient rinsing water flushes "everything" out.

up in the heads, since a small particle can return to the bowl through the toilet pump's lip valve. Hard urine deposits can also accumulate in the pump and pipe, which at first leads to a thinning of the inside diameter of the pipe and can eventually even lead to complete blockage.

Normal vinegar or vinegar essence is ideal for decalcification. Pour this liquid into the toilet bowl and pump it into the pump and waste pipe from time to time.

There it does its work all by itself and loosens the deposits. After a few hours for the solution to take effect, pump and flush the toilet well.

For electric toilet pumps, pump for around 10 seconds to completely flush the device.

Conclusion: When it comes to keeping the toilet in good condition, there can be no such thing as too much flushing.

How Deep is the Water?

This is a question that one never really has to ask on a yacht with built-in sonar. But even without looking at the indication device, one can often judge the water depth by looking at the course of the coastal formations. Naturally, this only serves as additional information to what the sea chart indicates.

Tip
If one is sailing along a flat shore or a wide beach, then there will also be a large area of shallow water. Keeping an appropriate distance is advised. If, on the other hand, there is a steep coast with vertical cliffs approaching, then these walls extend below the surface. On such coastal sections, individual rock outcrops reach up vertically from the depths and one should take special care to avoid these.

Generally, it can be said that the sea bottom falls off at more or less the same angle as the coast rises from the shore. Even so, this eyeball navigation can only supplement the study of the charts, since exceptions—in this case "nautical obstacles"—confirm the rule as always.

Sometimes it is better to trust your own eyes instead of digital indicators.

7. Comfort and Luxury

All Blue Towels Are Blue

Charter companies claim to value well-maintained and unified equipment on their yachts. It is not only the rigging, hull, and electronics that should be in good condition, the guest's towels should also look smart, be uniform, and in the company colors (mostly blue). And this is where the guest's problem starts: The crew jumps merrily into the water, the towels are hanging neatly in a row on the railing to dry, and when the first one comes aboard after the swim the puzzle begins: "Which one is my towel?", "Pass me the blue one!" come the calls from the swimming ladder. But which blue towel?

Tip

One doesn't have to sew on name badges or embroider respective initials or even write on them with a marker (which doesn't come out again by the way), but a small marking, a piece of tied-on whipping twine for example, can help to assure the towel's identification.

Upright Organization of the Book Collection

Especially on (extensively) cruising yachts, books and magazines of various sizes form part of the basic literature on board. Harbor pilots, travel guides, repair manuals, catalogs, and instruction manuals are just as essential as lighter and heavier literature, including word puzzles and soduku.

All these individual items have only one major drawback: When underway, at sea or in a seaway, they eagerly get mixed up and distribute themselves around the book shelf, sometimes throughout the entire cabin.

Tip

To keep books neatly in place, removable bars can be erected while in harbor. Or, less conspicuously, a bungee cord can be spanned in front. Tightly stretched between hooks, it effectively prevents the beautiful books from falling out.

To prevent the individual volumes from lying askew in the book cabinet itself, good old bookends come to use.

Nice and uniform, but easy to confuse.

Now nothing can fall over easily.

No matter whether it's made of wood, plastic, or metal, when the bottom has been lined with non-slip film, all books and magazines remain upright in their intended positions. And another tip: Non-slip or even screwed-on bookends divide the cabinet and also keep containers for spare parts, toolboxes, and similar items in check.

Deck Scrubbing with a Rinse

When it comes time to tackle the tedious task of cleaning the deck, the crew disappears with flimsy excuses, especially after a long mooring. Stubborn dirt and fine dust in every crevice requires the use of a deck brush or even a pressure washer, since simply spraying the deck off with clean water doesn't help much.

Cleaning is a must.

Tip

But pressure washers are expensive and require a power connection. If need be, the deck brush is happy with just a bucket. At the same time, using a hose to rinse the deck with fresh water dissolves deposits of salt crystals.

Unfortunately, the skipper seldom has three to four pairs of hands at his/her disposal to handle the hose and the deck brush at the same time. A few hose clamps or simple cable ties provide a solution. Use these helpers to attach the hose to the brush handle in such a way that the hose end points to the brush head. A continuously adjustable spray nozzle distributes the rinsing water exactly where it's needed. And the "deck-scrubber" can completely devote his/her time to the task at hand.

The Odds and Ends in the Cockpit

A skipper often has to suffer through all the little items that the crew leaves behind— above and below deck, in the cockpit, and in the salon. In particular, sunscreen, glasses, cookies, books, and cameras are always left lying around somewhere. In no time, the table and benches are covered with these odds and ends and you have to take care not to spray the cockpit with a long arch of sunscreen by stepping on it.

Tip

Collecting the items and having an auction for the benefit of the on-board budget is one creative solution to this problem. But simple and homemade pockets using sail cloth create instant order on board.

In order to make these you need a rectangular piece of durable material that is stitched around the edges. Fold the top 2" (5 cm)

Those who don't tidy up, quickly end up with chaos on board.

When one buys fresh eggs they usually come presented in an egg carton, which is made from recycled paper or even plastic. It is this egg carton that will be turned into egg cups. To do this, cut the carton up in such a way that one egg can fit into each of the individual egg holders. And just like that, egg cups have been created for the whole crew. The plastic version, in particular, is ideal for repeated use. The paper egg cup should be discarded with the egg shell after the meal.

With these easy-to-make egg cups, the breakfast egg stands up securely.

over loosely and line the top edge with a few snaps. This upper flap is folded over the top stanchion cable and secured with the snaps. If one adds strips of Velcro to the bottom edge, then this material can be folded over the bottom cable and secured using the securing strips. Of course, you should also stitch a second piece of material on in such a way that the desired pocket is formed. Here all the odds and ends on board can have a tidy place to live.

This sailcloth pocket is also useful for charterers, since the pocket can be adapted to any railing height with the flexible Velcro.

DIY Egg Cups Made on Board

Even when on board, many people don't want to go without their breakfast egg. Some want it hard boiled, others prefer the softer version. This requires an egg cup, which will be a hard find on most yachts. A resourceful skipper will also solve this "breakfast problem."

Ice Cold in the Fridge

Finally, your summer trip to the southern regions has started. It's not only decent wind that now pleases the skipper and crew, it's the well-chilled drinks that are enjoyed in abundance. However, the built-in freezer only cools when the motor is running. Since these heavy power consumers would otherwise suck the batteries dry, this places access to refreshments in conflict with the principles of stalwart sailing.

Cool drinks please the skipper and crew..

The only thing that helps here is ice in the refrigerator, whether as a solid block or as loose ice cubes. But where do you get such a luxury?

Tip

The first place to look for ice is the fishermen. And not the smaller boats that only go fishing for a few hours, but the larger ships—trawlers for example—that are often underway for days. Here an abundance of ice is needed to keep the catch cool and fresh. For this purpose, these ships board a large amount of ice blocks before going to sea. These are usually delivered from the factory by truck. When the skipper asks for a block, it is usually granted and the refrigeration on board is guaranteed for days. Sometimes the ice is free, sometimes a few cans of beer help, or a couple of bucks change hands.

If one cannot manage to procure some ice from the fishermen, then the next stop is the fishmonger. The fishermen will know where to find him/her. The desired ice can usually be found in the cold storage.

If that doesn't work, then supermarkets specializing in provision for yachts sometimes sell ice blocks or also plastic bags of cubes to the yachties—but at clearly elevated prices! Then there are also the cafe's and bars, which typically have ice makers. Here a pound of ice can easily cost several dollars—this commodity is getting expensive.

And if you work up a good bill eating dinner at a restaurant, you may be able to convince the owner to leave a few large bottles of drinking water in his/her freezer overnight. You can then bring the bottles on board at breakfast.

The ice block is the best coolant by far, followed by cubes. In last place for keeping things cool are water bottles. But the advantage with the bottles is that once they have melted, the result is cool and pure drinking water.

Another tip: Don't simply allow water from the melting ice to run off and away. This water is still a great way to keep things cool, as long as it still has some ice drifting around in it.

Fastened to the Rail: The Swimsuit That Can't Be Lost

This is typical behavior: The crew leaves the yacht for a swim and afterwards their wet items are hung on the railing. This is no problem with clothes pins, if they are available! But in the case of swimming trunks and other items of clothing, pins aren't necessary.

Secure swimming trunks without clothes pins.

In warm regions this is no problem at all, since the biggest swimming pool in the world is lying on the other side of the swimming ladder. But it has a drawback: It's salt water, and many people don't like this at all.

Tip

The bottle shower is ideal for conserving fresh water. Empty plastic water bottles can be re-used and filled with hose or tank water to serve as a mobile shower. This saves an enormous amount of water. Charter guests in particular can provide themselves with a little more comfort on board with this technique. Instead of using the deck shower and a lot of fresh water for washing away salt after a swim in the sea, simply use the bottle shower.

Using a bottle shower for rinsing is also essential during a visit to a deserted beach with no other possibilities for a shower. After the last swim in the sea before heading home, it feels good to rinse the salt off.

Tip

Simply place one leg opening of the swimming trunks over the stanchion cable and pull the rest of the garment through the gap between the cable and the material. The result looks like a wrongly tied clove hitch, as one often sees with fenders that are tied on to the railing. But in this case the laundry remains securely on the sea railing. Not even strong winds will blow it off and you've eliminated the need for having clothes pins on board, which aren't in abundance on yachts and very often go overboard.

Of course, other laundry can be effectively secured to the railing like this and kept from blowing away. The only question is how long the skipper wants to sail around with a traveling laundry line.

The Bottle Shower

Not every harbor has a water connection for regularly refilling the on-board water tank. But even so, the skipper and crew don't want to be deprived of a regular freshwater shower.

A small amount of fresh water goes a long way to feeling refreshed.

Put Shoes in a Basket

Deck shoes, as the name implies, should be worn on deck, and street shoes on the street. This prevents the marina's dirt, especially little stones that perforate the delicate deck surface with little holes, from coming on board. The best place for changing or removing shoes is on the side of the deck or at the end of the gangway. But what do you do with the footwear?

Tip

The solution is very simple: Give the shoes their own container. This shoe basket can be made of durable plastic or also out of wicker. Attached it in an easily accessible location, to the stern pulpit for example. There it is at a reachable distance when boarding or going ashore. Dirt brought along from the shore falls into the basket and can be discarded after time. If the shoe basket has a perforated bottom, then the sand and dirt can fall through the bottom, along with possible penetrating moisture. If the location is favorable, these will fall directly into the water without dirtying the deck.

A shoe basket helps to keep the deck clean.

A Poison Sprayer for Showering

Tip

The yachtie can find many practical things for on-board use in the local hardware store. In the garden department, for example, you can find pressure sprayers. In the garden these devices are usually used for applying weed and pest control. On board, however, the pressure sprayer is used as a very water-efficient deck shower.

A pressure sprayer helps save water.

Pour fresh water into the reservoir. After closing the lid, pressure builds up because of the integrated pump device.

Our deck shower is now ready for use. The spray head can be adjusted to produce a fine spray. This has two benefits: first, it uses very little water and second, the water cools down significantly when it is vaporized, making for an especially refreshing shower.

A Barbecue Grill for the Beach Party

Spending the evening in a secluded bay, looking out at the anchored yacht, lighting a fire and then grilling fish, meat, and vegetables while enjoying a glass of red wine is the ultimate for many boating enthusiasts! For the beach party to be successful, a few things have to be considered

Tip

Buy the grilling supplies beforehand, since nothing is more frustrating than finding the dream bay but not having anything on board to grill. Hours before the actual party, one can marinate the fish or meat with all kinds of spices and wrap the potatoes in a protective layer of aluminum foil so that they can be placed directly in the coals to bake (you should also include a pat of butter and some salt in the package).

But, of course, the most important thing is the barbecue grill, which should always be on board. You can buy simple, inexpensive grills in supermarkets. When the device consists of two separate grills joined by two rings, which acts like a hinge, then the two parts can be folded together. Place the meat in the middle of the two grills, so that it can be turned easily without the use of additional "tools." This also prevents the delicate skin of the fish from tearing.

If possible, the fire should be made far away from trees and grass and close to the waterline on shore. Arrange a few stones in the sand around the fire so the grill can be placed on them.

The crew can collect dry wood from around the area—this is more fun than bringing charcoal.

A little bit of paper, some kindling, bone-dry leaves, then a few thicker twigs, and finally a match, bring the flames to life. Thicker logs are to follow, but the fire shouldn't flare

There is always a grill at hand in the oven.

too high to prevent flying sparks. When a good amount of coals have been formed, allow the fire to die down. That's when the grilling can begin.

When heading back to your vessel at night, it goes without saying that everything that was brought to shore should be taken back with you. No rubbish should be left behind, and it is best to use disposable paper cups.

Don't cover the fire completely with sand, since the coals can remain hot for days underneath. Merely extinguish it with water. If you observe these points, you will enjoy a night on the beach that won't be memorable because you cut your feet on shards of glass or started a wild fire.

Bungee Cords as Spice Holders

On every yacht and on every boat, there are things that should be easily accessible to the crew, but these items, like spices for example, shouldn't slide or roll around, especially in a seaway.

Of course, you can store them in a locker or a container, but this will then disappear into a cabinet. The cook needs salt, pepper, sugar, thyme, etc. at his/her fingertips. That is certainly a solvable problem.

Tip

On many ships there are wasted corners in the galley: a small strip on the working area, behind or beside the lid of the ice box, stove, or sink. None of these spaces is being used for anything, but they are always accessible. This is exactly where the spices fit!

Using screws or hooks, span a bungee cord along the wall of the area in question and use this to secure the spices and salt and pepper shakers to the wall.

Bungee cords are very flexible and versatile.

Bungee cords of various diameters are available by the foot at marine outfitters. They are ideal for stowing and securing items on board. In the stern locker, for example, they keep fenders neatly pressed against the wall as well as lines and other equipment in their place. On deck, they strap down sails and boat hooks; below deck, they secure navigation equipment, toiletries, clothing, or just spices.

But bungee cords do have one drawback. They age very quickly under continuous exposure to sunlight on deck. They become hard, loose their elasticity, and have to be replaced.

Keeping Towels from Flying from the Stanchions

Many skippers don't like towels hanging on the railing at all. For them it seems sloppy and disorganized. But towels need a place to dry since they take forever to dry below deck. The railing remains the best place. Like on a clothes line, the towels flutter around in the wind, quickly becoming dry, which is very important, especially on trips south where one often jumps off the yacht for a swim and needs a dry towel within reach.

But, of course, the towel shouldn't be able to fly away in the first gust.

Tip

Depending on the size of the towel, place two or three clothes pins on the towel over the shroud cable from above. In strong wind, you can also place an extra few pegs on the sides. Thus, the important item stays where it belongs.

The towel is drying safely in the wind.

Home Remedies for Jellyfish Stings

Every summer, jellyfish will once more drift towards the coast and surprise many an unsuspecting swimmer with their stinging tentacles. If you feel a burning and stinging pain on your skin, it's happened. You have come into contact with a stinging jellyfish. Luckily, there are no types of jellyfish in the Mediterranean that can cause paralysis or death, but the poisonous tentacles still offer a painful red rash.

Tip
Acid helps when one has come into contact with a jellyfish. Pour vinegar or lemon juice onto the affected area as soon as possible after the incident, but don't rub it in. After a very short time the pain should ease and the water-born rash become less pronounced. Incidentally, vinegar also works well against insect bites.

A Sleeping Pad as Cockpit Padding

Seat cushions in the cockpit look good and increasing the comfort level is significant. But most are upholstered with artificial leather so that you can't sit on them in swim wear or your skin immediately clings to it. They aren't very hygienic either. And furthermore, the synthetic leather is usually filled with normal rubber foam, which soaks up moisture when wet and refuses to dry out.

Tip
I, myself, have had cockpit padding made that has a polyurethane interior. This material can be found quite inexpensively at camping outfitters as sleeping pads or mats. The great advantage of this material is that the foam doesn't soak up water. The additional benefits are that you can sit warmly and comfortably without it getting too hot in summer, the synthetic material is very stable, and the padding dries very quickly if it gets wet.

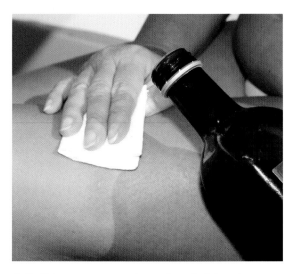

Jellyfish can cause extremely painful rashes.

Try using a sleeping pad for cockpit padding. It is light, warm, doesn't soak up water, and, above all, is cheap.

A cold fridge is indispensable in warmer regions.

Managing Cold Storage with a Refrigerator

An efficient refrigerator on board greatly increases comfort. Not only does it provide cold beer, it also extends the shelf life of provisions, which makes it easier to live in supermarket-less regions for long periods. You can, of course, install a high-performance cooling unit, but these devices require a great deal of energy, something that is not in abundant supply on board.

Tip

But with conscientious and effective "passive refrigeration management," you are one step ahead.

In many cases, you can add additional insulation, which drastically decreases power consumption. How the refrigerator is packed also makes a difference. If you buy your drinks cold and pack them in the fridge immediately, then the cooling device is sav-ing energy. If you leave a large water bottle standing for hours on the deck in the sun, it should be no surprise when the entire refrigerator heats up after placing the hot water bottle back into the fridge. When cruising without shore power, economizing the refrigerator's energy is necessary. Right after getting up in the morning, switch on the fridge so it runs for a while on battery power. Then, when sailing, the batteries are recharged by the motor. Of course, if you have sufficient battery capacity, you may be able to leave the unit running for the whole day of sailing. Otherwise, switch it off while sailing to keep it from draining the batteries. And when the ship's diesel is running again, the fridge can start cooling.

If it is exceptionally hot and the drinks need to be freezing cold, the skipper can sometimes buy an ice block from a fisherman, a fishmonger, or a supermarket. This will effectively cool the drinks in the fridge, as well as in the glasses.

Cleaning the Decks with the Morning Dew

Tip

Every morning is the same. The entire deck is wet with the night's dew. You could leave this layer of water to dry, but why not put it to good use for the yacht's upkeep. The dew is pure, fresh water, providing the skipper with a free resource for rinsing salt from the deck while washing it at the same time.

If the dew is wiped around the deck with a cloth, it gets rid of the sea salt as well as any dirt that has accumulated overnight. A rubber squeegee, the same kind used for window washing, can also be very effective here.

This method helps to keep the yacht clean anywhere that doesn't have a water hose available for rinsing the deck.

The morning dew eliminates the need for fresh rinsing water and saves time when getting the yacht ship shape.

Delicious Melon Punch Served in a Melon

Tip

Every skipper can spoil his/her crew with this fruity drink, and they'll thank you for it, because no one says no to a melon punch served in a melon.

You only need a few ingredients for making this refreshing drink:

A treat for the crew.

▶ 1 ripe watermelon
▶ depending on the size of the melon and the number and thirst level of the crew, a respective number of bottles of dry white wine and sparkling wine
▶ 1 Bowl
▶ 1 Knife
▶ 1 Spoon
▶ 1 Ladle
▶ 1 Pot

Place the melon in the pot, which will here serve as the "melon holder," keeping it from falling over. Using the knife, cut across the top of the melon to create a lid (see picture). Cut a small notch in the lid for the ladle handle to fit through. Hollow out the melon using the spoon. Place the pulp of the fruit into the bowl, where eager helping hands remove the seeds and cut the fruit into small cubes.

Pour the juice and about half of the pulp back into the hollowed-out melon. Then add a bottle of wine. The melon and the rest of the fruit goes into the fridge for a few hours along with the wine and sparkling wine.

You can also add a dash of brandy, Metaxa, plumb brandy, or the like for refining. If the punch is only supposed to be a fruity, thirst-quenching drink, then you can also add a some soda water to tame it.

The melon, wine, and sparkling wine should be chilled, or you can add ice cubes. To prepare it you simply add equal amounts of wine and sparkling wine until the vessel is full. When serving, places the complete melon on the table, covered with the lid and position the ladle so it is sticking out of the notch you carved. The clever container alone will astonish the crew.

Those who are really eager can cut the melon into slices after the beverage is imbibed and gnaw at the fruit remaining on the rind. It is advisable to go for a swim directly after this to rinse off of the sticky fruit juices.

Practical Addition: A Door Bell for On-board Visitors

Nobody likes it when visitors suddenly appear in the living room, unannounced of course, and possibly unwelcome.

Tip
The remedy on yachts of all sizes is the same as at home: equip the "front door" with a bell. On a yacht, the front door is the gangway or railing, which one can also open or shut. And one who wishes to board the yacht has to ring the bell. You can then "peep through the garden" and decide if you want to receive the visitor or not. Practical! Incidentally, door bells are also found on many mobile homes.

As visiting someone's home, ring at the door before entering.

Railing Seat with Cup Holder

Tip

Many yacht builders should consider this idea, it is simply marvelous! One has a great view of the yacht from a comfortable seat on or in the stern railing. While sailing or in the marina, or even at anchor, you can sit in it quite securely and it even has a backrest. As shown in the picture, the American yacht builders have already considered where the skipper would like to sit while thinking about his/her next journey and correspondingly bent the steel piping and formed a seat with wooden slats. On other yachts one can do-it-yourself by securing a triangular wooden plank to the corner of the stern railing. In order to provide the backrest with some slight padding, use a common insulation tube used on air conditioning tubes.

The special highlight in my example is the integrated cup holder! This is real comfort. An extra tip for those who would like to have such a seat on their boat: The distance from the opening of the cup holder to the horizontal pipe of the stern pulpit should be at least 5" (130 mm). This is the height of the average can.

Non-Slip Table Cover

Tip

That which works well in the trunk of a car can also do its job on a sailing or motor yacht. The non-slip trunk mat also keeps many things in their place on a yacht. Many accessories in lockers and cabinets get tossed around when the yacht dances up and down in a seaway.

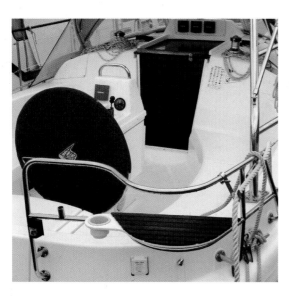

Where the skipper likes to sit.

With this non-slip mat, cups and glasses remain upright.

8. Supplies and Waste

Fishing Rod Mount from the Hardware Store

Fishing from on board is a pleasant pastime and fresh fish in the pan or on the grill is a delight. It is common to fish on board by trawling. With this method, a lure attached to a long fishing line is dragged behind the yacht when sailing. When a fish strikes, the line is carefully reeled in until the catch can be brought on board. But where can you keep the fishing rod so that—awkward as it is—it will be out of the way? The rod should be placed into a steady holder, which shouldn't interfere, the line shouldn't be able to become entangled anywhere, and the rod should also be quickly and easily accessible. Impossible to solve? Not at all.

Tip

One can find expensive plastic or metal rod holders at marine outfitters. But why should you spend money unnecessarily, when it can be made using materials from the hardware store for significantly less?

A nondescript grey drainage pipe with a 2" (50 mm) diameter and 20" (50 cm) in length costs under $10.

You also need two saltwater-resistant hose clamps with an inner diameter of approximately 3" to 3.125" (70–80 mm) for this DIY construction.

Using the hose clamps, attach the pipe to the railing at such an angle so that when placed into the pipe the tip of the rod will stick out over the stern of the yacht. And that's it, around $15 in material costs and about two minutes to adjust the hose clamp. The rod holder is ready. There can be nothing cheaper or more simple.

Extra tip: Placed over the end of the stowed rod, the piece of pipe also fits into the fishing bag of the eager fisherman.

Big impact for little money.

Simple Fishing Equipment

Fresh fish is always popular during the voyage and is sure to provide a culinary highlight of the trip. Whether it is grilled, stewed, fried in a pan, or made into fish soup, the crew's mouths will be watering when they catch the smell wafting from the galley. But where do you get the fish? One can, of course, buy the fish. Frozen in many shops, fresh from the fishmonger, even more fresh directly from the fisherman when he comes back from his/her fishing trip, or the freshest of all, when the fish is caught directly from on board. And, as is shown by the following example, the equipment doesn't need to be lavish or expensive.

Tip

To catch fish one should trawl an artificial lure—called spinners, wobblers, or blinkers—behind the yacht, attached to at least 165' (50 m) of strong fishing line. For reeling in the line, you can use a wide piece of wood or a plastic line holder, as can be found in

A round plastic line holder and a lure. This equipment is lightweight and easily packs into luggage.

fishing shops for a few dollars. On board, attach the fishing gear to a stern cleat. Here one winds the line around the cleat in such a way that if the lure is taken, the line will be released slowly, thus signaling that a fish is hooked.

The fishing line is then reeled in, the fish lifted onto the swimming platform and quickly dispatched with a hefty blow from the "priest," a winch handle.

Using this method in the Mediterranean, for example, you can catch mackerel, bonitos (a species of tuna), or even a dorado or a small dolphin. The fish often weigh around 3–5 pounds, thus ideal for a hearty dinner with the whole crew.

Incidentally: Due to its light weight the simple fishing equipment which is described here can also be carried in your airline baggage.

Easily Carrying Shopping Bags

Every cruising sailor knows this: The way to the supermarket is pleasant, but the march back with full and heavy shopping is torturous. The handles of the shopping bags cut into your hands painfully. After a while you can no longer feel your hands and the fingers are bent crooked.

Tip

A simple piece of wood or metal pipe provides significant relief when carrying heavy bags. Simply use a piece of wood or a round pole of at least 8" (20 cm) and pull the handles of the plastic bags over the edges. With your hand in the middle, even heavy bags can be carried painlessly without much effort.

In Africa, heavy items are carried using a much longer pole balanced on a shoulder.

Those who want even more comfort, can carve or file notches into both ends of the round poles to stop the plastic bags from slipping off.

But one often forgets these carrying aids at home, so use a piece of discarded wood lying on the side of the street. And if there comes an occasion where you have a lot of heavy things to carry, then one can use an African custom: Take a 3.25' (1 m) pole, attach your bags to the end and swing the pole together with the load over your shoulder! People carry their loads across great distances this way, why not do the same with our groceries on the way back to the ship?

Gas Supply in Croatia, Greece, Italy, and Turkey

Many yachts use gas stoves in the galley. They are easy to use, inexpensive, have a long life, and don't have an unpleasant smell. But the procurement of propane isn't always easy in every country and its harbors and marinas. Sometimes regulations prohibit trade in combustible substances, or many businesses simply don't have the concession to sell or exchange gas canisters. In addition, the distance to a gas supplier can sometimes be long and the travel costs involved surpass the value of the goods considerably. An on-board bicycle can be of great use here, by the way. But the real problem comes with the varying containers and their connections:

Every country has a different system for storing gas and not every gas station has an adapter that may fit your cooking equipment.

Tip

The most universally used is the so-called Camping Gaz. In many countries one will find varying bottle sizes with distinct connections. The bottles are simply exchanged, empty for full. Thus, one has to have bought at least one bottle, and after that the only charge is for the fuel—this is, however, markedly more expensive than local products, although the content is practically the same.

For owners who generally sail their yacht in the same region, rigging equipment with the local standard is the right choice. But those who are constantly underway will have to be satisfied with Camping Gaz bottles. Alternatively, you could install an alcohol or kerosene stove. In Greece and Turkey the exchange of gas tanks is very easy, since supermarkets and yacht chandlers usually have stock available. My tip: Don't make exchanges on weekends. The trip could be in vain, since the yachts that have returned on Friday and Saturday have already emptied the stores and the desired bottles are often unavailable out of season.

In Italy the tank-exchanging procedure is also problem free. The blue tanks can even be found in the Caribbean and Australia! And in Croatia one can have them refilled at

The same connections don't fit everywhere.

an official gas refilling station for cheap. But due to the danger of explosion, most of these filling stations lie outside the cities, so that it can be quite far away—and unfortunately not every small town has such a station.

If you have no idea where to find the fuel, simply ask the employees of any charter company! Their yachts are usually equipped for gas cooking and are thus regularly in need of gas and gas equipment.

Flattening Beverage Cans

This conserves space in the garbage bag.

Garbage is always a problem on board; it doesn't smell very nice and takes up a great amount of space. Even after a short weekend trip, a giant heap can accumulate, which is difficult to store. A large part of the volume is due to empty beverage cans, and squashing them takes some effort. Here is a tip for making it easier.

Tip

First, dent the cans twice at 90 degrees to each other. The can then looks like an accordion. Now take the top and the bottom of your can in your hands and squeeze. The result is a really thin piece of scrap metal that won't cut your hand and will keep any leftover fluid from dribbling out.

Crates and Baskets in the Fridge

These days a fridge or an ice box makes up part of the standard equipment of practically every yacht. Nobody wants to go without the luxury of chilled food and drinks. But many treats pass their expiration date

in the unobserved depths of the cooler, and in the case of the fridge, the contents love to spill over the cabin floor when it is opened in heavy seas.

Tip

One way or the other, this problem must be fixed. This method makes it easy to find and organize things. Stackable plastic crates or baskets, which fit the cooling space as tightly as possible, create order.

Plastic bins can be stacked and filled easily.

The cooling goods can be neatly sorted into these containers. Even open tetra packs don't spill, since they remain upright. A tight clothes pin additionally secures the corner of the packaging.

Baskets provide these two benefits: you can see from the side what the container holds, and the cool air can circulate. In crates and boxes that are closed on the sides, especially in warmer sailing regions, you can use an ice block as an additional cold source. This takes pressure off the refrigeration device (and provides ice for the long drink on the side). The melt water conveniently accumulates in the containers.

Tip: Don't pour this water out right away, since even the melted ice keeps its cool for a long time.

Compressing Plastic Water Bottles

Even at home, garbage takes up a lot of space. On yachts, the storage room for waste is even smaller, and to make things worse, supplies often come with additional bulky packaging material. Disposable plastic water bottles in particular take up an endless amount of space once they're empty. But you can compress them significantly as follows.

Tip

To compress plastic bottles, first open the cap and allow the air to escape. Then compress the bottle until the bottom of the bottle and the neck are nearly touching. Now the air is out. To keep the air from reentering, screw the cap back onto the bottle top. Instead of one and a half liters, the compressed bottle now only takes up around a quarter liter of volume in the garbage bag.

Compressing empty plastic bottles minimizes the garbage volume.

Minimizing Tubes

Space on board is a rare commodity, especially for those who are in the middle of a long trip. They must take care to use up the stored supplies completely. It thus has nothing to do with being pedantic or miserly when you try to use up the contents of all kinds of tubes in an efficient way.

Tip

When a tube—regardless of whether it contains mustard, toothpaste, or silicone—has been half emptied, it generally takes on an ugly form. The remaining content is then more or less divided between the folds and dents of the tube and cannot be completely extracted. When one tries to roll up the tube from the end, then the folds in the metal prevent it from being rolled up evenly. But these uneven areas can be ironed out in the truest sense of the word. For this purpose, the end of the tube is ironed from back to front over the edge of a table. Now, turn the tube over 180 degrees and repeat the process one or two times.

The content of the tube is hereby forced completely to the front and the now empty half of the tube is once again completely smooth. It is now easy to roll up the tube from the back. This looks neat and it can be emptied completely.

Above or Below the Water?

Where should the waste tank go? In the coming years, ever more countries will make it a requirement for yachts to be equipped with waste tanks. When fitting—and also when purchasing a boat—the position of the holding tank in the boat should be checked.

Every last bit must come out.

If it is incorporated in the keel, then it is indeed well stowed and out of the way, but if there are problems, it is virtually impossible to do any repairs there in the deepest part of the hull.

Tip

The question "above or below the waterline?" emphasizes an important aspect with regards to positioning. Each tank needs an outlet, through which the holding tank can be emptied at the harbor pump station.

In the case of storage below the waterline, there is the considerable added cost of an electric or manual waste pump. This technology is sensitive and needs to be serviced (how nice) and replacement parts are required from time to time. And in the case of a manual pump the delightful work must be done by hand.

If, on the other hand, the waste tank is placed as high as possible above the waterline, each toilet user pumps their own contribution up into the tank. The standard on-board toilet has no problem with the difference in height from one up to just below two meters. A one-way/lip valve has usually been installed in-line as a standard.

The advantage of this configuration is that one merely has to open the respective seacock (on the open seas), and thanks to gravity the tank drains itself without the use of additional manual or electric energy.

Taste Testing for the Water Tanks

Not every water tap provides true drinking water. And even if it is actually labeled as drinking water, that doesn't necessarily mean that it is really suitable for drinking—at least not in terms of its tolerability and safety for our stomachs.

Tip

Using appropriate decontamination tablets, or filters if it really comes out thick, the water quality can be significantly increased. It also has to be considered that the tap water could be coming from various sources. Fresh spring water or water retrieved from deep sources is usually of the highest quality. On islands, on the other hand, the precious liquid is either delivered by tanker, collected in cisterns, or sometimes also produced by desalination plants. Then it is first stored in tanks before it flows through the pipeline towards the consumer.

Generally, it is more or less treated beforehand. Usually it is decontaminated and made drinkable through the use of filters and chemicals. This, however, results in the tap water having the strong smell and taste of chlorine, or the taste is considerably affected by other additives. And

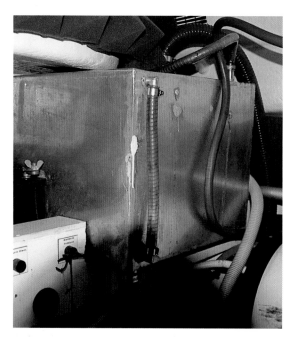

The height above the water level is what matters.

The taste test indicates the quality.

there is no way the yachtie wants to fill his/her tanks with such water! That's why performing a taste test at water bunkers is essential before the filling hose is stuck into the inlet!

Water Bottle as Transportation Container

It is truly a pity when carefully collected shells, coral sand, a cactus clipping, or the delicate souvenir from the tourist shop doesn't make the trip back home in one piece. In fact, they usually come off the plane crushed and destroyed. This doesn't have to happen!

Tip
A robust container for diverse holiday souvenirs is available in the form of a disposable plastic water bottle from the supermarket. It is truly stable and can be sized for various transportation measurements. For this purpose, one first cuts off the conical upper part using a sharp knife, the souvenir concerned can then be placed into the empty plastic bottle section, it doesn't matter if the bottle isn't filled completely. These can be padded with kitchen towels if needed.

The knife can be used to cut the bottle cylinder to the required height. When everything is finally stored, the lid (thus the previously cut-off top section of the bottle) is placed back on. The top and bottom parts are connected using a strip of adhesive tape. Packed in this way, even fragile items survive the trip home without damage. If you place this transportation bottle in your hand luggage, you can be fairly certain that its contents will make it home in one piece.

Even delicate souvenirs can be safely packed in plastic water bottles.

With many items, the length of a single water bottle doesn't suffice—with plants, for example. Take a number of these plastic bottles and cut off the top and bottom sections, thus leaving a hollow cylinder. Using tape, attach the parts together until reaching the desired length.

One upper and one bottom section now encloses the tube. You can also tie a lanyard to the top and bottom, then it can be casually swung over the shoulder, leaving both hands free for other luggage.

Where to Take on Fuel in Turkey and Greece

It's not only the water supply that can often create tricky problems for the crew to solve in eventful ways—the procurement of diesel, and even more so gasoline, can also be difficult. Those who are used to having a gas station around every corner are bitterly disappointed. Filling stations directly on the water are only found in a few well-equipped marinas. Once the trip is underway, the crew sometimes has to be resourceful in order to get the tanks filled up.

Tip

Small tanker trucks with diesel sometimes pass up and down the marina in the afternoon, waiting for the sign for a fill up. This is very practical, since the yacht doesn't have to be moved, but receives fuel directly at its berth. For mega-yachts, there is even a massive articulated truck that comes to quench the engine's thirst.

The harbor master or local tavern owner usually knows where to reach the mobile fuel supplier. There are no such services in small fishing harbors. It's not rare for a single service station to supply an entire island.

Unfortunately, this one station likely doesn't lie on the water, but somewhere in the interior. For the crew this means a pilgrimage to the gas pumps with the reserve canisters! On the islands, the taxi is *the* means of transportation, thus also for the diesel cans. For the taxi driver, such trips are nothing unusual, even if he has to make multiple trips to and fro until the tanks are filled.

If the gas station owner has time—and this he usually does or at least seems like he does—he sometimes helps with the diesel transport using his/her vehicle.

In many harbors the mobile fuel supplier comes to the yacht.

If necessary, the island bus will have to be used for the transfer. Ingenuity and improvisation lead to success.

Changing Money in Turkey

Vacationers in Turkey have many opportunities to acquire some Turkish currency, the Lira. The first, and probably the most expensive, is through your own local bank. Here you can order Lira beforehand and take it with you on the trip to Turkey.

The Euro is accepted almost anywhere in Turkey.

The quickest version of the currency exchange is at the airport on arrival. Go directly to the exchange counter after entering the arrivals hall to change your home currency. Most new arrivals first go looking for a luggage cart, then go and wait at the luggage conveyor, and only once they have collected their luggage—after some waiting—do they move on to the exchange counter. In the meantime, a queue has formed.

The cheapest way to change money in Turkey is at the post office. At towns and villages with post offices, you'll see the PTT sign displayed at the entrance, and find the best exchange rates.

In distant markets one pays in the local currency.

9. Mooring and Casting off

Mooring Solo with Land Lines

Many solo sailors, who have made their home on the world's seas for many years, have difficulty during harbor maneuvers. Often the yacht, which is so efficient out at sea, is difficult if not impossible to control in tight spaces. This brings to mind many a robust long keeler.

Tip

But you can also make the process easy. When you are supposed to moor using the bow anchor and move with the stern between two yachts into a tight gap, the solo sailor can drop the anchor exactly in front of the berth while slowly sailing past it. Here only enough chain is let out to hold the yacht for a short time. Next, use your tender to go to the allocated berth and tie on a long line, the other end of which you will return to the yacht.

With this secured to the stern cleat, you can now very slowly, but very surely, move closer to the dock wall by paying out the anchor and hauling in the long line. This maneuver also works in unfavorable winds.

Mooring Alongside

As long as the wind is only blowing lightly, there is nothing wrong with mooring to the windward side of the dock. But if there is a possibility of the wind picking up, then one should leave it and look for another berth. The maneuver itself isn't difficult to perform.

Sometimes it simply becomes too tight for single-handed mooring.

Well prepared: fenders, lines, and crew.

Mooring with the Bow to the Pier

Those who like to see everything ahead of them or who have problems with reversing can, as solo sailors do, also move forwards into a gap and bring out the stern anchor.

Tip

Here the fenders are brought out on both sides—just below the toe rail—and two bowlines are prepared on the foreship. By prepared, I mean that the end of each is secured to the cleat and the rest of the line is passed underneath the stanchions to outboard and then back over and laid down in loose loops on deck. The yacht is now positioned in front of the gap, sails towards it, and when an appropriate distance from the wall is reached, the skipper lets the stern

Tip

Depending on the available berth, the skipper maneuvers his/her yacht more or less close but parallel to the dock wall and keeps it in this position. This can be achieved by carefully moving forward and backwards. The wind will then slowly but surely push the yacht to the dock, allowing the skipper to bring out his/her lines and secure the yacht. Preparation for this entails the proper fender placement on the side of the hull that will be moored so that no scratches occur.

Sailing forward onto the dock is easier.

anchor drop into the water. Here care has to be taken so the chain doesn't run over the gelcoat and that the anchor doesn't end up lying across the neighbor's chain.

Keeping light tension on the anchor line with one hand and the tiller and throttle in the other for keeping the direction, the single-handed sailor slowly sails his/her yacht into the gap, secures the anchor, and can then tend to the bowlines. All this with only two hands as a solo sailor? It sounds more complicated than it is, since the rudder and engine throttle can generally be handled with one hand.

Mooring with a Bow Spring

Not every skipper has a run-in crew for his/her trip, or many prefer not to have one at all. They are forced or even choose to sail solo. The big problem usually doesn't start while at sea. In order to be able to safely handle the yacht in all conditions, it needs to be rigged for a solo sailor and above all needs a good auto pilot, to keep a straight course. Only when arriving in a bay, or truly when entering a harbor, do some of these solo-sailing, old salts experience problems, since he doesn't have enough hands for handling lines, anchor, and yacht at the same time. Despite this, the normal mooring maneuvers under normal weather conditions should be manageable by a solo sailor, provided a careful and foresighted plan has been made.

Tip
Depending on the maneuver, this includes, for example, that the anchor, fenders, and lines are made ready and even positioned and sail tied in a sort of "basic position" that serves for most maneuvers.

Springs are practical when mooring and casting-off.

This avoids hectic running around on deck while the yacht drifts around without helmsman in a perhaps tight and overcrowded harbor mouth.

Going alongside seems to be the easiest choice of mooring maneuvers for solo sailors. Once the fenders have been distributed and adjusted to the appropriate height for the dock, and the bow and stern lines have been secured on the cleats and made to run fair, one can slowly and carefully maneuver and bring the yacht to a halt at the dock wall. Then it is no longer a feat to jump over the railing and secure the mooring lines on the dock. If there is a passer-by available to help on land, then this is even easier. Once the yacht is safe and secure, the skipper can rig the lines to slip and secure them on board. Thus, when casting-off, he can manage all the lines from on board and has no need to go ashore to release them. Finally, he rigs a bow and stern spring and the yacht lies nice and secure in its berth. If a side wind is complicating the maneuver, the solo pilot can secure a bow spring on the bow cleat and lead it back to the cockpit outside of the shrouds. In this way, he can cast the line from the cockpit to a (hopefully) available bystander and ask him/her to secure the line on land. The skipper can now use this line to pivot the yacht and thus bring the hull against the wall. With the motor in gear, low revs, and the rudder turned towards the dock, the yacht will now remain stable in this position, allowing the soloist to go ashore himself to secure the remaining mooring lines. The motor can then be switched off.

Casting Off with the Bowlines

Those who plan to stay on the dock wall or jetty for a long period will have brought out enough fenders along the entire length of the hull beforehand. The bow and stern lines are secured for this. Two crew members are briefed in advance on the procedure for bringing out the two mooring lines. In the picture, it is easy to see that the bowlinesman has moved back to the level of the shrouds with the bowline led back outside of the stanchions, since it is here that the hull is at its widest and the dock will come the closest—thus an ideal spot for jumping onto land.

Keep in mind: Always keep a hand free for yourself.

The fact that this crew member can hold onto the shrouds with one hand also helps. In the other he should have a neatly coiled line bundle, preventing the mooring line from tangling, which could cause the maneuver to go wrong.

He has one leg already placed over the railing on the side of the hull, since only in this way can he take a wide step without running the danger of his (oilskin) pants getting caught in the stanchion cables. What won't work, however, is if the crew member with the bowline—or those with the stern lines—remains on the bow or respectfully the stern, waiting for the moment to be able to jump off, since the hull will come closest to the dock somewhere around midships and both crew members will be waiting in vain for their chance to get off.

Boat hook lashed to the bow pulpit using bungee cords

Boat Hook for the Bowline

Handling the yacht on the open sea is no problem for the solo sailor. Only when mooring in the harbor can things become tricky. The various actions have to take place simultaneously: helming to steer the ship, bringing out the fenders, preparing the lines, etc. etc. etc.

When everything is finally prepared, the soloist needs to be ever-present at the stern, bow, and helm. So it is very nice when, while going alongside, the bowlines lie prepared on the foreship and a helper is standing ready on the jetty. But his/her arms won't be long enough to reach the mooring lines.

Tip

The problem is easily solved. Using the boat hook as a long arm, the single-handed skipper can hand over the bowline to his/her helper very easily.

This is how it works. The boat hook is attached to the foreship area—to the bow pulpit for example—in such a way that it extends over the side of the yacht at a right angle. The loosely coiled bowline is led over the end of the hook (secured to the bow-cleat!). When the skipper now carefully goes alongside the jetty, the on-land helper can reach the prepared end without contortions, take up the bowline, and secure it on land.

The Lines Are Off

With the passing of time, the ropework on any yacht becomes stiff and no longer as easy to handle. This is partly because of exposure to sunlight, which causes the syn-

Washing the lines also super-cleans the dinghy.

Fenders Attached Using a Clove-Hitch

I always find the most interesting knot constructions made by my fellow sailors when it comes to tying the fenders to the stanchions. From truly fascinating, highly complicated creations, which are virtually impossible to undo, to minimalist versions which cause the fenders to be lost immediately.

Tip
The clove hitch is a knot which is easy to learn and to tie and holds under every condition. It is also easy to undo when the fenders have to be moved in a hurry.

thetic material to become brittle and start to crack and partly because of salt, which crystallizes inside the line and makes it stiffen. The mooring lines also collect all sorts of dirt from bollards, the dock wall, and posts, which makes them look unsightly. The only solution is a wash day.

Tip
The tender can serve as a large wash tub that has space for all the on-board ropework, itself being cleaned in the process. If possible, it is filled with a mix of lukewarm freshwater and a biodegradable detergent. The lines are then placed inside and left to soak for a few hours. During this time, as with normal washing, it is continually moved around, squeezed and twisted. Finally, the water is drained and freshwater is used for rinsing. The clean lines can now be wrung out and hung on the railing to dry.
Incidentally: Regatta sailors like to throw sheets and trimming lines in the water to wet them before the start. Wet lines are suppler and can be handled more easily than dry and stiff ropework.

The clove hitch: durable and easy to tie.

When things have to go very quickly, one should add a slip to the clove hitch beforehand, this makes for record-time knot releasing. And those who don't trust the holding capability of this simple knot can add a half-hitch for safety.

Placing a Foot on the Stern Line

The most tense moment of the mooring maneuver must be when the boat has stopped, and is thus unable to be controlled, and the mooring lines are transferred to land. The lines now need to be pulled through as quickly as possible to bring the boat back under control.

Tip

Usually there are bollards or rings available. With bollards, it is simple: one simply puts one or two turns around the bollard and even a large and heavy yacht can be held using one hand. With rings, things are more complicated and tedious. One has to feed the entire length of the line through the ring before the yacht can be kept at bay.

Those who try to control a large yacht by merely holding the line in their hands will soon find out that this doesn't work. But one can control the boat by putting as much body weight as possible on the line. At the same time, both hands are free to work the loose part of the mooring line through the ring. The more one weighs, the more the boat can pull on the line.

Shortened Stern Lines on the Cleats

Surely you have experienced this before. A yacht sails into the harbor of its berth, an eager helper is standing ready on the dock, and on board the crew also has the mooring lines in hand, ready for the transfer. The lines are then cast with a lot of momentum and often all at the same time. And then it happens: the helper is overwhelmed by the countless feet of mooring line!

He now starts the search for the end of the line and, after finding it in the giant tangle, feeds it through the ring, which is indicated through loud and clear gestures by the crew, since the line is needed on "slip" A.S.A.P. In

It is recommended to practice hauling the line through when one has a quiet moment.

Shortened stern lines on the cleats make things easier for the helper on land.

the meantime, the yacht is drifting free in the water—usually back away from the dock.

Now it could also happen that the helper discovers that an unexpected knot has suddenly brought the feeding through to a halt. By now, the yacht has drifted onto the neighboring vessels and the crew members are hectically shooed to the railing to fend off. It now often comes to the game so loved by owners— "bend the stanchion," since a lot of pressure is naturally put on the railing supports involved—those of the neighbors of course.

Back to our friendly helper on land. He is now lying on his stomach on the wall and has finally undone the tangle. Now he can at least feed enough line through the mooring ring to be able to hand or toss it back on board, if there is still someone there to receive it. If so, the mooring lines are now taken up on—possibly with the help of a winch—coolly and as if nothing had gone wrong.

The dirtied helper has already been forgotten. There you go—it worked!

Yes, this is a version which is happily practiced again and again. The alternative is to secure only as much stern line to the cleat as really needed, before starting the maneuver. Then the helper's job is made quite simple and stress free, and the crew also benefits.

Fender on the Stern

In the Mediterranean, it is common to moor with the stern to the peer. When a crew member then brings out the stern lines and needs to go ashore to secure them, the skipper has to go quite close to the shore in order for this to succeed. This however also means that the yacht hull has to be brought to a halt at only about a half a meter's distance from the pier. If this doesn't succeed, then the stern will hit the solid wall with a terrible crash, leaving at least deep scratches, if not an ugly hole in the hull.

Tip

A stern fender can prevent this. But the measure only works if the right stern fender is used for the particular yacht in question. On a vertical transom, a normal fender will do, if there is no swimming ladder, weather vane, or other protruding part that would require the use of a larger diameter fender.

In which case a large-diameter ball fender would be appropriate. But if the yacht's tran-

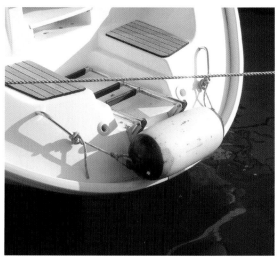

Various preventers offering protection against the dreaded bump on the dock.

som falls off at an angle, then a "normal" fender won't help, since it would only slip up the slope and the yacht would touch the harbor wall in any case.

On many yachts, a large ball fender will be able to prevent the worst. It is also very helpful when one is lying alongside and wants to bounce on the bow or stern spring when casting off.

Bringing Out Long Land Lines

Many anchorages are so small or popular that not all yachts can swing freely on their anchors. The room for this is simply too limited. For this reason the yachts lay their bow anchor and then attach one or two long lines to trees or boulders on the shore.

Here the yacht lies safely in its anchor position..

Two different maneuvers can be used for this to succeed:

▶ Using the tender: the yacht drops the bow anchor ahead of the desired position and then moves back carefully towards the shore. The dinghy was brought out beforehand and is now in standby position. In both cases the windward land line is brought out first. If the distance from shore is not too large, the long lines can be tied on board and then the other end is dragged to a position to windward by the tender crew using paddles or an outboard, and secured there. The lee line is brought out next, and after that the yacht lies comfortably, securely, and in a way that saves space.

▶ Using a swimmer: the land lines are, as with the dinghy version, laid out on deck beforehand, free to run. The swimmer's end is tied into a small bowline loop, which he/she can pass over his/her arm. He/she now has two free hands for swimming and climbing onto the shore. On the skipper's command, the swimmer jumps in and secures the stern line on shore. The bowline loop helps to quickly form a large loop, which will tighten on itself when placed around a boulder.

In each case the land line should be well prepared, since a tangle would quickly result in a failed maneuver. The yacht should furthermore be held tight on the anchor line by engaging the reverse gear. If this isn't done, the weight of the chain will pull the hull away from the shore and the dinghy or the swimmer will have to cover an ever-longer distance dragging an ever-longer line. With the tender version, care should be taken so the outboard will have no bottom contact, which would result in the shearing off of the safety shear pin or damage to the propeller. Contact of the dinghy with sharp-edged stones could also cause serious damage. Incidentally, the version with the "swimmer" is by far the fastest and safest.

Long Bowline Loop

When it comes to the question of whether the mooring lines should lie on slip or whether a bowline on the bollard or ring on shore is the right choice, opinions are divided. Having the lines lie on slip has the great advantage that they can be handled from on board. But, they have to be twice as long as a line that is secured simply. One who secures their yacht on shore using a bowline when casting off is faced with the problem that a crew member has to undo the knots—and this on the land.

Tip

A "longer bowline" provides the solution! Simply make the bowline-loop, which is placed around a bollard on shore, big enough so the knot of the bowline can be reached from on board. In this way, a crew

Almost like a slip line.

member can comfortably undo the mooring lines from deck and no crew will be left on shore, once all lines have been released and the yacht sets off.

Coiling Lines Properly

Many mooring maneuvers take a sudden and unpleasant turn when something goes wrong with the lines. The crew members trusted with transfer of the lines cast them towards the shore with all their force, but before they reach halfway, they plunge, fully tangled, into the water. This problem has various causes and can be avoided in many ways.

Tip

Lines can, of course, be coiled up on hand and elbow, then tied into a bundle and stowed in a corner of the stern locker. But they can also be coiled in even loops on one's hand. This is achieved by lightly twisting the line between the fingers—for example coiling to the right and twisting to the right. The end of the line is wound around this line bundle a few times, then the last piece, of just under a meter, is doubled and pushed through the upper "line bundle bight," and the end is then pulled through the resulting loop. This remaining end of the line can be used to hang up the line on the stanchions for drying using a clove hitch, for example, or for stowing in the stern locker.

When the line is needed, it is easy to find and ready to use. One always reaches through the line bundle and then you undo the lashing. Now the end is ready for use.

Without forming knots, it can also be cast over a long distance, depending on the length of the line, since the individual loops uncoil themselves during flight, preventing the often-seen line-casting tangle.

If the line is properly coiled, it can be thrown to land without tangling.

Connecting Lines Using a Double-Bowline

It often happens that the length of a line doesn't suffice. For example, in Turkey or in the Caribbean, where the yachts lie on their bow anchor and secure themselves to the shore using one or even two long stern lines. Here 65' or more is needed to secure them to the land at low tide. Often enough, the lines are too short for such a maneuver and need to be extended.

Tip

For such cases, the textbooks recommend a reef knot for lines of equal diameter and the sheet bend—simple or double—for lines of unequal strengths.

These work very well, so good in fact that these knots are practically impossible to undo afterwards, especially when great tension is put on them after having gotten wet, which is inevitable. When a line gets wet, it becomes very supple. Under tension, such a knot is really compressed, and if this knot then dries out, then this line connector is nearly impossible to undo.

If, on the other hand, one uses two interlinking bowlines, then the problem described doesn't appear at all, since a bowline is easy to undo even after great tension has been applied.

And this doubled-bowline also has a secondary benefit. Because of the considerable weight of the (wet) knots, they also work as a small counter-balance weight, preserving lines, yacht, and the skipper's nerves.

A doubled-bowline is rock solid and easy to undo.

Maneuvering with a Double-Engine Setup

Catamarans are also always very popular in our regions, with both owners as well as charterers. Compared to an equal-length keel yacht, they offer double the width. This means that almost double the space is available on deck, in the saloon, and in the cabins. There are no tight V-berths and even in the aft cabins there is generally enough headroom. Even at five on the Beaufort scale, the drinks remain standing on the table, and—most importantly—catamarans have two engines, one in each hull.

Many larger sailing yachts and many motorboats and yachts also have a double-engine system.

Maneuvering with a double-engine system works just like operating a tank.

one doesn't need to use the helm since the direction of movement is controlled via the throttles of the two engines. As with large motor-yachts with double-propulsion, one travels backwards with pin-point accuracy merely by controlling the two throttles. During the maneuver, a short forward pulse with one engine can be used to make a large change in course or reduce the speed.

It is quite normal if this doesn't go quite so smoothly the first time, which is why when going out for the first time, every catamaran beginner should take a little time to practice going in reverse in some quiet corner of the harbor (something that should be done with an unfamiliar mono-hull as well!). Those who have built up some confidence in this way will maneuver the wide multi-hull confidently and without stress in tight harbors, and maybe more accurately than with a mono-hull.

Thus, they offer the same maneuvering properties as the catamarans. A double-engine system offers unexpected maneuvering characteristics, which is why many sailors avoid chartering a multi-hull, since they don't know how the handling with two independent motors and props works. But maneuvering with a double-engine system isn't at all so complicated.

Tip

The two motors can be controlled independently from each other. Similar to a tank, by putting one engine into forward and the other into reverse, it is possible to turn on a dime. When sailing forward, a cat behaves similar to a mono-hull, except that one can choose to use only one of the motors in order to save fuel.

When sailing in reverse, the positions of the rudders aren't even important, because

Drying Wet Lines

In practically every mooring maneuver, the mooring lines are inevitably dropped into the water and are brought back on deck sopping wet. Now one can't just leave them lying around the deck to dry, nor can they be stored in the stern locker. Here the drip water would create a lovely humid ecosystem below deck.

Tip

I hang wet lines on the railing until they are dry, only then are they stowed away. For this purpose the lines are first coiled up properly and the line end pulled through in such a way that there remains at least 1.5' hanging free. This 1.5' can be tied to the stanchion cable or the bow or stern pulpit in a clove hitch. If you want you can add an extra half-hitch to the end as a precaution.

Those who dry neatly coiled lines on the railing avoid creating a humid ecosystem in the stern-locker.

Mooring to the Buoy in Reverse

Fields of mooring buoys can be found in various regions: in Croatia, Sardinia, in the Caribbean, and in front of the Whitsunday Islands in Australia. They are usually placed in areas where the sea bottom—in conservation areas for example—is to be protected from the anchor gear of yachts or where resourceful businessmen charge fees for the use of the buoys. In either case, many find it practical to moor to a buoy. But making a line connection is not always easy.

Tip

Many buoys already have a strong floating line attached, which simply has to be fished up by a crew member using the boat hook and secured to the bow cleat. Often one has to feed one's own line through the shackle, which is situated below the buoy; this is a drag in the case of yachts that have a high

bowsprit. So why not pick up the buoy there, where you yourself are as close to the water as possible, and forget about the awkward boat hook?

One can take up the buoy from the stern, while standing on the swimming platform, quite comfortably and without effort.

To do this, the helmsman maneuvers towards the buoy with the stern into the wind. It is much easier than having to keep the unstable bow into the wind at low speed. Once having reached the buoy, one carefully halts to prevent it from being driven away again by the prop-wash. A crew member, yes even the helmsman himself can do this, secures the yacht to the buoy with a mooring line that is set to slip, and not to the stern, but to the ship's bow, and led back on the outside! The buoy can now be released and the stern of the yacht will swing around until the bow has turned into the wind. If the bowline is too long, it can now be adjusted from the foredeck. Some attach a second bowline to the buoy with a bowline or as a slip, in case one of the lines is chafed through.

With this trick, the days of tugging at the buoy, especially in stronger winds, are in the past.

The line needs to be at least one boat length.

10. Boarding and Going Ashore

Using a Ladder as a Gangway

When looking for a gangway you may find yourself in the hardware store. Of course, the marine outfitter offers a wide variety of manual and automatic solutions, most of which cost a lot of money.

Not every region requires the use of such a piece of equipment. But in the Mediterranean, for example, one usually uses the "Mediterranean mooring," thus mooring with the stern to the dock. In this situation a gangway is indispensable, otherwise one would never get to land.

Inexpensive, robust, and stable: the aluminum ladder modified into a gangway.

Tip

Your hardware store offers an inexpensive solution in the form of an aluminum ladder. It is cheap, doesn't rust, is robust, and very light. But, of course, you can't walk on it yet. Also in the hardware store you will find water-resistant plywood, which can be cut in such a way that it fits between the two rails and rests on the rungs of the ladder. Water-resistant plywood is cheaper than marine plywood and will last for many years, since it doesn't come into direct or constant contact with water. The plywood should be about 0.5" thick. You can also join two thin pieces with epoxy—this is even more robust.

Once the pieces have been fitted, then we can tentatively screw them onto the rungs. Once all the required holes have been drilled, the plywood pieces are removed one last time. Both the sides are then brushed with epoxy resin.

After drying, the process is repeated one or two times, ensuring the pieces are well sealed. The plywood can now be screwed to the aluminum ladder permanently. Finally, one brushes the sides one last time, in order to protect the screws as well. Your new gangway is ready!

DIY Bow Access

When sailing, you often see yachts being moored with the bow to the peer and the crew has to scramble over the bow pulpit to get to shore. And if the bow is also quite high and the pier especially low, then this can turn into a dangerous climb, especially for older sailors who are no longer very flexible.

Tip

Many owners remodel the bow pulpit of their yacht without further ado. If the bow pulpit is open in the front, one can comfortably disembark from the bow without having to climb.

If the bow pulpit is widened, then you no longer have to worm around the forestay. If it is modified to extend forwards over the yacht's bow, then the yacht's hull doesn't need to lie quite as close to the pier—an additional safety aspect. A grating on this platform ensures a solid grip, without negatively affecting the seagoing qualities. The anchor can also be directly integrated into this platform. And the rail of the bow pulpit provides a great railing for getting on or off board.

Retractable gangway at the bow.

Retractable gangway with swimming ladder steps.

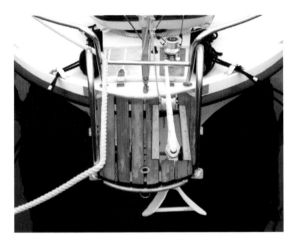

Pulpit with a broad cross-cab.

Fancy: hydraulic, pivoting gangway.

Bow Gangway Construction

As easy as mooring to the pier with the bow may be, just as difficult can be getting on shore and back on board over the bow. When the pier is very low, then this maneuver can turn into a real climbing exercise. One often sees beer cases turned over on the dock wall in an attempt to minimize the difference in height, but this is an accident waiting to happen. This is why you will find a simple bow exit construction described below.

Tip
A short spar is lashed in the bow area at a right angle to the midship line, to the bow cleats, for example. Attach your gangway plank to this. The other end is placed loose on the pier. Swell or even changing tide levels won't affect this set up. To get on shore or back on board, simply walk over this plank—the bow pulpit even provides a hand railing.

The Hovering Gangway

Unlike the north, where yachts are either moored alongside, in rafts, or with the bow in berth, in the Mediterranean one moors using the bow anchor and with the stern to the pier.

Getting on shore and back on board can become a climbing exercise.

The gangway is a proven aid for getting to shore. On the one hand the yacht transom is protected, since some distance is maintained from the pier, and on the other hand such a gangway is also comfortable for getting on board and on shore.

Tip

In the most uncomplicated case, a simple plank which reaches from the transom to the dock wall will do its job effortlessly. A lanyard, which is secured on board, prevents this *passarela* from being lost. Real gangways are more comfortable, one side usually fits onto a swiveling deck fitting, the other end hangs from a line which often leads to the top of the mast, keeping the plank on level with the pier. Mobile rollers provide good traction.

On big and expensive yachts, one can also find hydraulically driven luxury devices with integrated indirect lighting together with a red carpet, which are controlled by infrared remote control and come out without rope support, but we won't even mention these.

If the gangway rests on the pier and the yacht moves, then noises that disturb the night's peace are inevitably caused. And the constant scraping on the ground doesn't do the boarding device any good. But if a sturdy bungee cord is tied between the gangway and the height-adjustment line, the onshore end of the *passarela* can be adjusted to hang, hovering approximately 8" (20 cm) above the pier. If a crew member then wants to get on or off the yacht, the bungee cord stretches and the gangway comes into solid contact with the pier, allowing them to pass over the plank safely and comfortably.

When there is no longer anyone standing on the gangway, it goes back into its automatic standby position, hovering above the pier. Broken gangway rollers and interrupted sleep are a thing of the past.

Without a gangway, getting on and off the yacht becomes difficult.

Non-Slip Gangway Plank

You can go one step further to refine the homemade gangway. Make it skid proof. Of course you could buy the available anti-slip paint or material and brush or paste it onto our gangway. But you can also create your own non-slip layer.

A non-slip gangway ensures sure footing.

Tip

For this project you need epoxy resin, which you already used for the ladder gangway, as well as some sand.

You can get your sand from a beautiful secluded beach, but some welding sand from the hardware store or bird sand would also do the trick. The gangway plank is brushed with fresh epoxy. Then sift natural sand through a flour sieve (bird sand is already purified) and carefully distribute onto the wet epoxy resin. Excess sand should be discarded. Merely turn the gangway over to get rid of the loose particles.

The synthetic compound should then be left to dry. In order to increase the durability, another thin layer of epoxy can be added. After curing—usually overnight—the clever item is ready for use, and there can be no more complaints about having "slipped" on the slippery gangway after the evening's trip to shore.

What to Do with the Gangway When Not in Use?

Whether it is a large aluminum gangway or a simple gangway plank, only on large yachts can it remain mounted on the stern. After casting off, smaller yachts need to dismount and store the awkward item. Because of its size, the important item usually doesn't fit into the aft locker. Lashing it to the transom—whether standing on end or lying straight across—is usually not considered, due to either practical or aesthetic reasons. Lying flat on deck, the device poses a threat to the toes, besides the fact that lines and sheets could get caught on it.

So what do you do with the gangway?

Tip

One practical solution is to lash it to the railing on its side. The simplest and best way to do this is using two strong bungee cords, which are tied to two adjacent stanchions using durable clove hitches. Lanyards do not work quite as well for this, because when they get wet the line starts to stretch, causing the gangway to become loose and slowly but surely free itself. Then a crew member will have to go to the bow in heavy swell to prevent the important item from going overboard.

The gangway, standing on its side, is lashed leaning onto the stanchions from the inside using bungee cords. These are fished to the inside from beneath the plank and led up. The tensed bungee cord is attached right above the plank using a spirited clove hitch.

Another Version of the Gangway

Almost every yacht is unique, and every owner finds his/her own solutions for his/her vessel. This includes going ashore and coming back on board. One skipper solves the problem by using high-tech equipment and spending serious coin, the other finds surprisingly simple solutions.

Tip

In this gangway version, the owner has simply used a wide gangway plank, which, using a short strop and two shackles, has been hung to the protruding bowsprit. The onshore end has been attached to a bollard using a lanyard, preventing the plank from ending up in the water. But despite this the yacht can still move, since the attachment is flexible. Here it is important that the plank should be wide, so that it won't tip over.

In this way the gangway can be securely stowed: lashed to the stanchions using short strops and clove hitches.

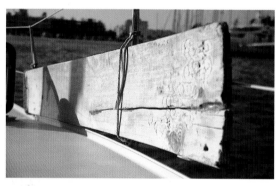

It goes quickly, is durable even in heavy seas, and is easy to undo.

Crossing from the yacht to land.

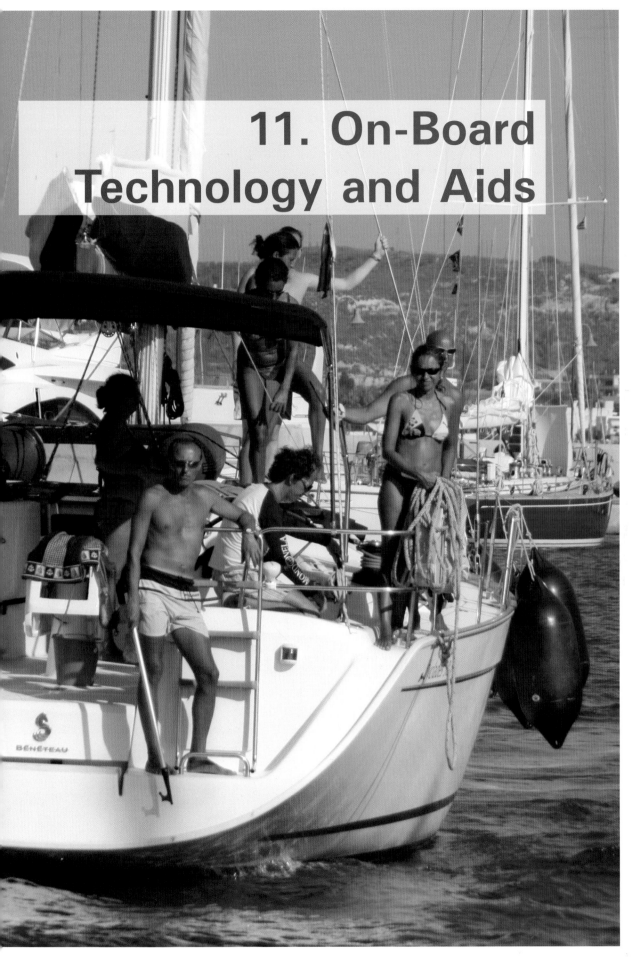

11. On-Board Technology and Aids

A Bag for the Paper

The toilet pump is surely one of the most sensitive parts of the ship. At the same time, it is also the device on board that is least eagerly repaired (after all it requires a gas mask, rubber gloves, protective suit, and rubber boots). Were it otherwise, not every sailor would know the saying: "I'd rather be up to the elbows in used oil than have to take apart the toilet." Here are a few tips on how you can reduce maintenance and repairs to the toilet.

Tip

To completely avoid things reaching the problem stage, used toilet paper should be thrown into a separate plastic bag, which is regularly disposed of on land. For this purpose a small rubbish bin lined with a plastic bag is simply mounted in the immediate vicinity of the toilet bowl, assuring a functional toilet lasts for a long time.

As a secondary benefit, it prevents the otherwise pumped and shredded toilet paper from ending up on the sea floor like fresh snow, which doesn't make for a very exhilarating view when swimming or snorkeling in the anchorage.

Toilet paper is also collected in separate bins in the toilets of pubs in many Mediterranean countries—this is by no means a new idea. Despite this, adaptation of this custom has been surprisingly limited.

In addition, toilet paper, empty toothpaste tubes, sanitary towels, cotton, personal hygiene products, hair, razor blades, and bits of soap do not belong in the toilet bowl, but in the described bin, which can be regularly emptied with the rest of the rubbish.

And another tip. In order to keep the pump in a working condition, a splash of oil in the bowl and a few pumps in order to distribute

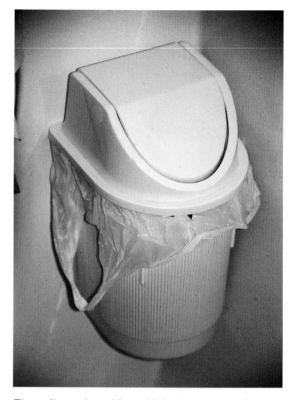

The toilet refuse bin, which is mounted right next to the toilet.

the lubricant will usually suffice. The oil to use is motor oil, or even simple baby oil. The toilet pump and waste pipe can be cleared of built-up deposits using coffee machine cleaner, which should be left to work for a few hours.

The Good Old Block and Tackle

In sailing circles, this term is, of course, harshly frowned upon, since a "block and tackle" could possibly be used on a building site, but certainly not on a luxury yacht. Of course, "purchase systems" do have their

Purchase systems offer great force with little effort.

use on board, being composed of high-tech "blocks" instead of vile pulleys.

Here the principles are the same. Energy efficiency is achieved through the multiple relaying of the line, which is directly proportional to the amount of relays and respectfully also the length of line which is required. In practice, this means that through the use of a single block, which is attached to the load, one only needs to lift half the weight, but the line required needs to be twice as long as the lifting height. This is actually known as the law of leverage, which we can still remember from school.

Tip

Even on board our modern yachts we also use purchase systems in various places:

▶ Thus, there is a block attached to the head of the mainsail, in order to halve the force needed for the setting of the large canvas This technology is especially used on catamarans and yachts with battened mains.

▶ The mainsheet is also rigged as a purchase, so the mainsheet trimmer can control even the large forces acting on the main in strong winds, using just one hand.

▶ The traditional *boomvang* is likewise composed of a purchase system, providing the great force needed to prevent the main boom from rising, thus stabilizing the mainsail's profile.

▶ The backstays on many yachts are also rigged as purchases, in order to give the mast the right bend and provide the forestay with enough tension, which leads to greater height when sailing on an upwind course. Sometimes there is even a second, smaller purchase rigged to the end of the large backstay with the purpose of increasing the purchase ratio, and thus the available force. Here, purchase ratios of more than 1:20 are no rarity.

▶ Or, one can use a purchase for fine tuning trimming lines, or simply to lift the dinghy up to the davits or to hoist the outboard up or down by means of an outboard hoist.

Of course, blocks with wide roller diameters, and preferably with built-in ball bearings, are the option with the least friction, therefore they need the least applied force—they are also the most expensive versions. For simple tasks or when things have to happen quickly and there is no block available, feeding the line through a normal shackle can also do the trick.

A Seawater Filter Can Work Wonders

Many people wonder why the engine's water-cooling pump impeller has to be changed so often. The main cause is dirt. The water-cooling pump is one of the truly important components for insuring the engine lasts. If it stops working, the first thing to happen would be that the coolant warning light on the engine control panel would light up—an alarm may start beeping as well. Here, quick action is required. Pull back on the throttle and, better yet, stop the engine completely. Since there's no more cooling water flowing through the engine block, it could be over in no time. The beautiful yacht engine would be gone.

This is why the water pump's impeller deserves special attention. This component is made from rubber and looks like a small paddle wheel with five or more paddles that force water through the engine. If these rubber paddles were to break off, the performance of the pump would be greatly reduced and the broken-off pieces of rubber would be washed through the finer coolant channels, where they could easily become stuck and cause further problems.

Different filter styles.

Tip

A seawater filter helps the beleaguered impeller have a significantly longer life span, since it collects all the larger dirt particles, such as shreds of seaweed, sand, and stones that would normally decimate the rubber gear.

To avoid the engine compartment from flooding every time it is opened for inspection and cleaning, the seawater filter has to be mounted somewhere above the waterline.

The filter inlet is connected to the seacock; the outlet to the water-pump.

No matter whether it is a direct or indirect cooling system, the impeller, and thus also the engine, will thank you through a significantly longer life span.

Mooring Line on a Chain

In many harbors, the bollards and rings available for securing our mooring lines are so dirty or jagged that we don't want to loop our lines around them at all.

Please don't throw it! The fixture between the rope loop and the chain is known as a thimble.

Either they become dirty in no time or the ropework is chafed through and your expensive yacht is left floating in the harbor.

Tip

Italian marina neighbors of ours had an idea for this. Splice a thimble (term for a metal loop) in to the end of the mooring line. Thread a 3.25' to 5' (1–1.5 m) piece of chain through the eye, which can be attached to a ring with a powerful carabiner. The chain easily handles the chafing on the bollard or ring. Our mooring chain has another benefit. When mooring lines are cast to helpers on shore, most of them don't know how to tie a proper knot or they have difficulties handing the line back on board as a slip. With the chain, none of that matters, since handling the carabiner is easy.

But be careful when casting the line to the pier. Don't aim for the guy on shore!

Fire Blanket for Interior Fires

Although one might prefer not to think about the possibility of an on-board fire breaking out at all, the old saying also applies here. Prevention is better than burning down.

As in many other areas, retailers offer many solutions for this problem. From the simple powder extinguisher, like those found in cars, up to fully automated fire extinguishing systems, there is a perfect match for every wallet and ship size.

However, powder extinguishers have the disadvantage that the extinguishing powder penetrates into every corner and thus after successfully extinguishing the fire, the most extensive damage is that which was caused by the powder.

Carbon dioxide extinguishers as well as those filled with simple water aren't suitable for use on all fires. And due to their environmentally damaging gas content, halon extinguishers have been banned for years.

But there is another way to be prepared: the fire-extinguishing blanket.

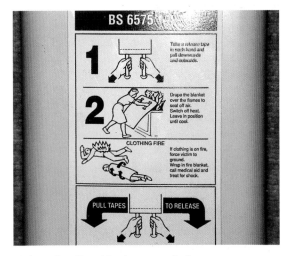

Using the fire blanket, small fires are put out quickly.

Tip

Fire blankets are made from fire-proof and non-permeable material. They are stored in a practical container that can be attached to a cabinet wall. In case of a fire, on the stove for example, one would pull on the protruding grab strap, unfold the blanket, and place it over the fire. The flames are thus smothered. If a person's clothes have caught fire, wrap the person in the blanket together with his/her burning clothes. The fire blanket is an effective extinguishing device for small interior fires, causing no additional damage beyond that caused by the actual fire.

Wing nuts would work well here.

Wing-Nuts: When Things Get Tight

So many owners are close to despair when it comes to fixing something in the tight engine compartment. You can't reach anywhere properly and you have to contort your body while holding wrenches, nuts, washers, and C-clips in your hands and all this while trying to work. On hot days and perhaps even out on the water in a rolling sea, this can quickly turn into a nightmare!

Tip

You can save yourself a lot of acrobatics in the engine compartment using simple wing nuts or wing bolts instead of normal nuts, which require the use of wrenches or socket wrenches.

This work needs to be completed once, but as a result, in the future you will be able to tighten and loosen comfortably with one hand, even in hard-to-reach corners.

Wing nuts are ideal for anyplace where a relatively small force is needed for tightening—the water pump cover, for example. Here the owner needs to change the impeller from time to time. This rubber gear often gives out at the most inconvenient moments

when the engine is sorely needed. And then one has to go into a contorted body position to replace it. But if the pump cover is secured with wing nuts, you can almost open the pump with one hand—even in an inaccessible place.

But wing nuts are not appropriate for places where the nuts have to be fastened with force, or where a torque wrench is prescribed. They are ideal and preferred for the water pump, electric installation boxes, fitting of boxes, and inspection holes for waste and water tanks. Here they save effort and the tiresome "fiddling."

Separate Circuits for Engine and Other Electronics

Electricity on board is certainly not a luxury. But the loads, thus the required capacities, are always increasing, and when the power for the additional electronics is taken from the starter batteries, it leaves the engine with too little power and it will quickly quit and go quiet.

Tip

This is why on many yachts there are separate batteries installed for starting and for the rest of the electronics. There are various ways of charging both sets of batteries together, but when the main engine is switched off, the two power circuits should be completely isolated from each other.

▶ The easiest way is through a mechanical switch. When the skipper turns it, he/she switches both batteries to be charged — thus when the engine is running—in parallel, and when the motor is stopped, he separates them again. In this way he can choose whether to switch battery one or two to be used as house batteries. If he/she remembers...

▶ Isolators are a proven technology that can do this job automatically. But the voltage drop caused by these components results in the on-board batteries not being completely charged.

▶ One could also consider two separate alternators, which would provide the two completely independent power circuits with power, but this would be an extra strain on the motor.

▶ The easiest way is to install a battery separation relay, a product used by the auto industry for decades. This relay is wired in such a way that it automatically switches on when the charging light goes out after starting the marine diesel. If it is stopped, the relay is also switched back off. The way it works is as follows: When switched on, both sets of batteries are simply connected in parallel. All batteries are charged at the same time. When switched off, both power circuits are once more cut off from each other.

With separate power circuits, you avoid situations where the engine doesn't start because someone left a cabin light on that drained the batteries.

Bungee Cord as an All Around Help Line

On every yacht there are constantly things that need to be tied down or secured. This is why many helm pedestals have lines of

With two power-circuits, the diesel always starts.

Bungee cords belong in a skipper's locker

Hand or Foot Pumps Save Fresh Water

On board, fresh water is precious. The water tank capacity on board is usually too small, but larger tanks are too heavy and would slow the yacht down. Regardless of how big the tank is, the crew simply uses too much of the valuable liquid.

Tip
An additional hand-, or even better, foot-pump effectively saves water, since one only pumps exactly as much water as one really needs. In the case of an electric pump, the water is running while you are still busy applying soap to wash your hands, for example.

Of course, no one should go without the benefits of a pressurized water system—this luxury is especially appreciated when washing dishes or showering—but the many times when only a small amount of water is really needed can add up. With a manual water pump, the water is dispensed according to need.

The pump is connected to an extra branch of the water connection between the water tank and the pressure pump.

various diameters hanging on them, ready for use.

Solid, durable, yet still easy to undo connections can be made using simple bungee cords.

These straps can be bought ready for use at hardware stores complete with incorporated plastic ends, that can be used to string multiple bungee cords together.

The performance metric for bungee cords is based on how little they cost and how much time they save.

Tip
Bungee cords of various diameters are available at marine outfitters. A small piece of wood can be used for one end. It should be approximately 2" (5 cm) long and have a hole that corresponds to the diameter of the bungee cord drilled in the center. Feed the bungee cord through this hole and secure it with a figure eight knot. Tie the other end into a small bowline. Items can now be fastened using the bungee strap. The piece of wood is stuck through the bowline and the strap is secured in no time.

Fresh water isn't always readily available and is therefore a precious commodity on board.

It has its own outlet, in the galley for example. An additional manual water pump provides water from outboard directly to the sink, where used dishes can be pre-rinsed and freed of the worst residues. And all this without having to touch the on-board water supply.

No More Puddles

On diesel yacht engines there is a thin hose next to the coolant filler cap that drains overflowing coolant when the engine heats up. Unfortunately, this pipe usually just runs into the bilge. This means that an ugly puddle is always formed in the deepest point. This is a nuisance, since at every visual inspection of the engine, the skipper should empty the water with much effort and then dry the bilge until the next time. With time, the once-radiant, spotless white bilge will take on an ever-more yellowy tinge, which is practically impossible to reverse.

Tip

The remedy involves a simple, but solid, plastic container, into which the end of the overflow hose is fed. To do this, drill a hole into the container's cap that is approxi-

In this way the bilge remains snow white.

mately the same diameter as the hose. The hose should be long enough to reach about 2" to 4" (5–10 cm) into the container, so that it can't slip out accidentally, which wouldn't be a catastrophe, but would simply cause the aforementioned bilge puddles.

The container itself can be secured in an accessible location in the engine compartment using cable ties, a thin cord, or some other means of attachment. One could also consider using a can or bottle holder, like those mounted on bicycles. Then, the loosely held container could easily be removed and emptied. If the collection container were made of a transparent material, you can easily monitor the level. Otherwise, the shake test can tell you how much water has been collected. Cost of material: Only a few dollars.

Line for a Broken Fuel Cable

No yacht is safe from accidents happening. From time to time, something always breaks, usually exactly when the appropriate replacement part is far away. This is where a talent for improvisation is called for; for example, when the Bowden control cable of the throttle breaks, which happens frequently.

Tip

This glitch cannot be fixed with the materials available on board. The entire control cable needs to be replaced, since the broken steel cable cannot be re-joined.

Despite this, the yacht can still continue, you just need to install a temporary control cable. A thin line will do the job.

For this purpose, unscrew the broken control cable from the engine and connect the line in its place. Using appropriate guides—

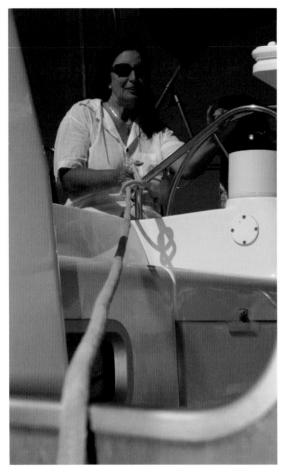

If the throttle's Bowden control cable is broken, an auxiliary line can quickly be rigged.

blocks are ideal, but shackles, carabiners etc. will also do, but with greater friction—lead the line from the engine compartment up to the cockpit.

With a little bit of luck, one might even be able to shut the engine compartment without catching the "fuel cable." In an emergency, you could drill a small hole for feeding the line through.

And then, tug on the line and the motor has full throttle!

It would also be great if the revolutions could remain constant without always hav-

ing to keep the "fuel-line" in hand.

This can be achieved by running the line through a cam cleat.

One solution using an ordinary G-clamp works very comfortably. Clamp it onto the helm pedestal or other appropriate location. The G-clamp functions as a throttle. Throttle is supplied by pulling back on the clamp. If the G-clamp throttle is moved forward, the revs and thus the speed are reduced.

The line might have to be led through the aft locker or over the stern to the cockpit. The most important thing is that the engine can be controlled from deck. Then one doesn't need to have a spare parts dealer right around the corner.

Milking Grease for the Underwater Hull

It's no secret that anti-fouling is quite expensive. The unlucky owner may easily have to fork out more than $100 for the yearly coating. And then there is also the issue of environmental conservation, since the more effective the anti-fouling is the more it is prohibited in certain areas.

Tip
Resourceful owners have been making use of milking grease for some time. This product can be gently applied to the hull using a cloth, a glove, or even a bare hand. A single coat is enough. This saves time and effort, which means that the job is completed in no time.

Lately, even the relevant sailing magazines have been reporting more and more about this wonder substance, and practice proves them right. Milking grease is ideal as an effective, biologically harmless anti-fouling agent, seeing as algae cannot settle on the slippery material and barnacles or mussels

Milking grease is ideally suited for the underwater hull. Only when it comes to hoisting does one have to take care so the hoist straps don't slip off.

cannot get a solid footing—they are easy to remove by hand if one tries.

Of course, this product also has its disadvantages: If the yacht is still standing on land after applying the milking grease, everyone who comes into contact will get it on their hands or clothing. When hoisting, crane operators are overjoyed when their straps end up covered in milking grease residue. In fact, when hoisting, you have to be especially careful the straps don't slip on the surface, allowing the yacht to fall out of the crane.

This can be prevented by using lines to attach the straps together on the left and right, perhaps even around the keel, in order to stop them from slipping. And there's something else which shouldn't be overlooked. If one touches bottom even slightly, then the beautiful coat is gone! So the milking grease isn't suitable for those who like to be laid up from time to time. But for those who have enough depth in their area and aren't planning to test the stability of their hull, a switch to this cheap and environmentally friendly substance is well worth a try.

11. ON-BOARD TECHNOLOGY AND AIDS

Oil Change with Pump

When it comes to our cars, changing the oil is relatively simple. The plug at the bottom of the pan is removed and the oil comes pouring out. Or, at the service station the thin probe of the suction pump is fed into the dip stick pipe and all that's left to do is press a button. The situation on board looks quite different from a car! Because of the cramped space, you often cannot even get at the plug at all, not to mention trying to place an oil collection pan underneath it. And then one would have to carry this shallow container through the entire yacht, at risk of spilling the entire contents.

Tip
The better option is sucking out the oil using a small hand pump available at many retailers for about $25.
There is also an electric version. As on a car, you feed the suction tube into the dipstick opening and diligently pump out the oil into another container. But you may want to have more than one pair of hands to hold the tube, pump, and container to avoid any spills. A few simple cable ties ensure that, in future, the dreaded oil change will go quickly, easily, and without contortions or spilling. The skipper simply uses these cable-ties to attach the small oil pump directly to the engine. The hands are then left free for other tasks. Many engines have an additional small access to the oil pan. You will find an approximately 0.5" (10 mm) diameter hole somewhere in the vicinity of the dipstick pipe.
This hole is closed off with a plug. The plug is replaced with the suction tube, which can remain there permanently. Now the only thing left to think about is a practical container for holding the used oil—a used

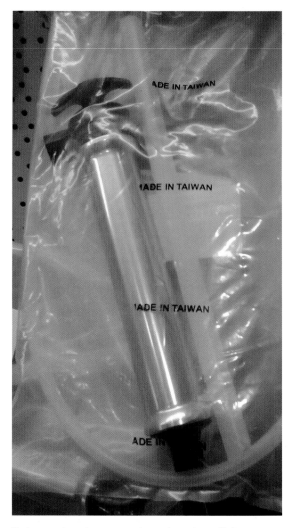

Using a hand-pump, changing the oil becomes child's play.

water bottle works perfectly for this.
Once the small pump and suction tube have been installed, the oil change can be done in no time. In the future, the skipper will be much more eager to do an oil change, since the tedious procedure will no longer include the unpleasant job of cleaning the engine bilge. The engine will also show its gratitude for the fresh oil with a long life span.

Clean Bilges Thanks to Dish Soap

Somehow there is always dirt of some kind in our bilges. Crumbs, hair, dust, and condensation water, and in many older yachts, this may also include drain water from the shower, some engine oil, or even diesel. This colorful mixture, of course, finds its way into the deepest corners of our ship's cellar and, thereby at least partially, escapes removal by cleaning rag or sponge. Below deck, a somewhat moldy odor starts to set in. If diesel is also added to the bilge brew, then after inhaling this smell, the rest of the crew delight the skipper by getting sick.

Tip

A fast-acting and, at the start of charter trips, eagerly used method is squirting a good amount of normal dish washing liquid in the accessible areas of the bilge, followed by a bucket of fresh water. Now, the crew can cast off and do a trip without too much heel, which ensures the bilge mix doesn't end up inside the closets. During this trip the rinse water will spread, reaching every corner because of the ship's movement, which loosens the worst of the dirt.

After a few hours of cleaning time and back in the marina, pump the bilge water off into a bucket or a similar container and properly disposed of it, especially in the case of oil or diesel contamination.

If the bilge is now also quickly wiped over with a rag, as extensively as possible, then the lemony freshness of the soap will provide for a pleasant scent below deck.

Here a cleaning is called for.

Making Line Curls

Attractive and practical, this is what can be said about line curls, the rolled up ends of lines.

On many yachts one sees neatly curled-up lines on deck. Many skippers claim to refrain from these line curls because they are supposedly impractical, but I personally believe these people are just too lazy to roll them up neatly. In fact, making line curls is child's play and very quick to do.

Tip

It is best to move the loose line bundle into the cockpit. Start the curling on the side deck from the end of the line. Roll by roll, the line curl gets bigger and bigger and by keeping light tension on the line it creates a tight package, which is very useful if one

The line curl: attractive and practical

Those who prepare for coming into the harbor in good time won't end up in a panic later.

needs to move it a little (or if one wants to use it as a doormat).

Such a line curl always looks attractive and the entire deck is tidied up. And when you need to use the line again, just roll it out from the outside so it won't tangle.

Bow and Stern Lines and the Cleats

When well prepared, things on the jetty also go smoothly. One, often enough, observes the following when yachts enter into a harbor or marina. The yacht comes sailing in, the skipper and crew look out for an appropriate berth, which is then found. The skipper thus aims for the gap, and right before the yacht reaches the jetty or pier, he starts to think about the so-urgently needed lines for mooring. Action now comes into the game. Aft locker is opened, scrambling for the mooring lines, which are guaranteed to be lying at the bottom, and then the lines are secured to the cleats in a panic.

In the meantime, the skipper has aborted his/her approach, because things took too

long. When the yacht finally comes close to the pier, the crew casts the mooring lines in the direction of the dock wall with vigor, but after only a few feet the now-tangled bundle of line falls into the water, along with all hope for a successful mooring maneuver.

Tip

Bow or stern lies should be led to the cleats from the outside, beneath the stanchions, and there secured with a figure eight with a locking turn. The figure eight on a cleat is to be chosen above a bowline or similar solid knots, since it can also be released when under load from the outside to the cleats, so the line doesn't end up across the stanchions and, in the worst case scenario, bend or tear them clear off.

If the line is coiled in proper loops, then the roll of line can be cast over even large distances and the flying end reaches the shore without tangling.

If the mooring lines are long enough, then they can be passed back on board from the pier, and there secured on the cleat with a figure eight with a locking turn. Advantage: When casting off, there is no need for a crew member to undo the knots on the shore and then use his/her last strength to jump on board the already departing yacht. Even a small crew can comfortably handle the lines from on board the yacht.

Secondary Speaker for the VHF Radio

All seagoing ships, and this also includes yachts, must ensure a continuous listening watch on the VHF calling and emergency channel. This is what the rule states. In everyday operations the device is needed to communicate with lock and bridge operators and even sometimes to discuss the traffic situation with other ships—thus who gives way to whom when in a tight traffic situation.

Listening closely sounds all well and good, but it's easier said than done. Since the radio device is usually installed in the vicinity of the navigation area, it is far from the ears of the helmsman, who should be able to listen to the radio traffic so that, if the need would arise, he could send a crew member—who has a radio license—to the radio.

Tip

One option for solving the problem is turning the radio up to full volume, thus assuring that it can also be heard in the cockpit. But this cannot be guaranteed to work in strong winds or with a running engine, not to mention the noise below deck.

Another option is to install a second speaker in the cockpit.

The speaker itself has to be waterproof. It doesn't need to have great sound properties, so it won't cost much. It can be turned on and off with a switch. Now the radio traffic can be followed from the cockpit, comfortably and well understood.

Staying in the loop when at the helm.

Despite cellular phones, a sea radio is necessary.

12. Skipper and Crew

What to do When You Lose Your Passport and Money

Every vacationer's nightmare is the moment when they realize his/her wallet or personal documents have been lost or stolen. Quick action is called for when travel documents, cash, and credit cards have disappeared.

If one has taken proper precautions, the loss won't be so bad. It is best to keep only a small amount of cash in your wallet. Travel documents and ID should be kept separately and preferably stored in the hotel safe for the duration of the holiday. You should make copies of the documents before the trip and leave a set of each with friends or family at home and keep one in the suitcase. Pin and emergency numbers don't belong in a wallet either.

Before leaving for the trip, you should also make note of important phone numbers, including your travel insurance provider, the number for blocking one's account, and the local number of the closest embassy or consulate where you are traveling. But what should or can you do in case of an emergency?

Tip

The first thing to do is contact your bank and inform them about the loss of the credit or debit card. You should always carry the appropriate number with you. The loss should also be reported to the local police for later reference. If traveler's checks were included in the wallet, they will be replaced by the local bank.

If you lose your passport or ID, it is best to contact your country's passport-issuing agency or your country's local mission. Usually the consulate department of the embassy in the respective country provides temporary replacements for lost travel documents. But these may only be valid for the journey home and have a maximum validity of one month.

Quick action is called for when travel documents, cash, and/or credit cards have disappeared.

The Convergence Behavior of Yachties

It is towards a solitary anchorage somewhere in the Mediterranean that we are steering our yacht. As far as the eyes can see there are no other yachts on the horizon. The bay is large and wide, and the anchoring depth in the Turkish lagoon-blue water is around 20' deep.

The bottom all around offers a good anchor hold. Your gear slips over the bow roller and from above you can see the anchor touching ground and the chain being laid out on the sand—perfect!

Where there is already one, there is space for another.

The engine is off, there is peace and quiet, you reach for your towel, strip your clothes off...but WAIT!...you yank your swimming trunks back up, because another sailing yacht is coming around the corner to contend for our paradise. Gone are the chances for skinny dipping, since of course the newcomer doesn't look for an anchor spot in some other area of the bay. Instead, he anchors directly up wind of your yacht, so that when swinging he comes dangerously close. His/her stern is only about 15' away from our bow! So what's happening with the anchors? Is there perhaps an anchor tangle? There are literally hundreds of feet of space, and there is really no need to be cramped.

And soon another yacht rushes in. Has word about this anchorage bay gotten out? This yacht comes to lie parallel to you on the starboard side. When swinging on the anchor you can almost greet the new neighbor by hand. So as a precaution we take out the fenders, one never knows.

In the distance you can see more yachts and boats heading towards "our" bay, and after about half an hour you find ourselves surrounded by an entire fleet of yachts, who are lying in a bundle as close to each other as possible, even though there is truly enough space for all. And when an excursion boat with sirtaki music blaring from its voluminous speakers and screaming pleasure trippers also decides to join, you decide you've had enough. You pick up anchor, but very carefully, since we now have to circle the yacht in front of us. You leave this place and try to find another bay that is so small that only one yacht, your yacht, can fit inside.

But why is there this herding behavior? One possible explanation is that if someone is already anchored somewhere, then it must be good and safe. This is why most people think they must try to get as close as possible. If the chains then cross each other or the hull sides touch, it comes to bad judgment of the skipper, who should have ensured a free-swing radius when placing his/her anchor.

Tip

The only remedy against this herding behavior is the already described measure: find yourself another space in another, hopefully peaceful, smaller bay. If this isn't possible, then you have to try to overlook the excitement around you with as much equanimity as possible and make the best it. Perhaps it could even happen that one meets nice and like-minded contemporaries on some other vessel in your anchorage, with whom one could end up spending a pleasant afternoon or evening.

The Boat Boys of the Caribbean

Every Caribbean sailor knows the boat boys. These teenage boys and young men seek out incoming yachts and gladly offer their services in exchange for hard currency (dollars). They offer to tie stern lines to the palm trees on shore, etc.

In particular, you will find them in the middle and southern parts of the Caribbean island crescent. The further south you get, the more aggressive the fight for the coveted stern lines becomes. This often takes place

as follows. A yacht enters a bay with, as is customary in the Caribbean, the dinghy trailing on a long line from the stern. Long before reaching the anchorage, a young man approaches in a skiff, paddling like crazy, trying to get the yacht to stop through shouts and gestures. If this measure doesn't succeed, he keeps on steering his nutshell towards the passing yacht and throws himself into the tender, without losing hold of his own little boat. Thus, he receives a free ride into the bay and the prospect of the palm tree job. But be careful. There have been cases where the boat boy was injured during this risky maneuver (perhaps even faked). In any case, the skipper is liable, so don't allow such behavior to take place in the first place.

Upon closer approach to the anchorage a whole bunch of other boys on similarly bizarre devices come closing in around the yacht. They hang onto the side of the hull together with skiff, surfboard, etc. and try to secure themselves the job. Mostly there is no other option than to give one of the youths the job, which instantly focuses the fury of the others upon him. The more impoverished the island, the more intense the reactions, which can sometimes even lead to wild insults between each other. Don't be put off, it's all part of the ritual, even if an outright fight or small sea battle breaks out. The job can only be given to one, and the empty-handed boat boys will soon turn their attention to the next incoming yacht.

But each one still wants to have a chat and offer their additional services to the skipper or crew. They try hawking mussels, snails, and handicrafts, guarding the yacht and/or tender during shore excursions, grocery shopping, supplying fresh bread the next morning, organizing fruit, fish, crayfish, or a taxi.... Anything is possible—for a fee of course—otherwise none of these services can take place. Skipper and crew have to consider that the "appointed" boy will simply buy the bread rolls from a supermarket around the corner and add a quick hundred percent for the trouble. But for this, one gets the exclusive service that anything desired is delivered directly to the yacht.

Many vacation yachties are intimidated by the sometimes admittedly pushy manner of the boat boys, but with mutual respect the cooperation works just fine.

Tip

It is important that the skipper nominates only one of the boys as helper and makes this clear to the crew and other boys. Business as well as mooring maneuvers should only be done through him. He is given the line, and once the line is secure, he also receives his fee (usually five to ten East Caribbean Dollars). Of course, he also wants to be nominated for the palm untying the next morning, but this can be left open by the skipper. After the chosen one and his colleagues have had the opportunity to promote their wares and services, the skipper can then explain to them that he and his crew now want to be left alone and require some personal space.

In my experience, the throng then slowly starts to dissolve in order to wait on the next yachtie customers and the crew can enjoy their holiday.

Avoiding Theft

Even if it isn't a pleasant topic, it must be addressed, because theft on yachts will always occur, even in so-called "civilized" regions. There are truly impoverished people, also refugees, who earn a little money through pilfering—entire gangs systematically rattle tourist hot spots to obtain mobile phones, laptops, cameras, jewelry, and other valuable items, which they then sell outside the country.

Boat boys do business with the yachties.

Sometimes a bankrupt circumnavigator needs a new tender or some other piece of equipment for his/her own boat...

A yacht is very easy to open. The companionway sliding hatch poses no challenge for one with long fingers, neither does the hatch cover. In southern regions these will often enough be left open in order to ventilate the yacht interior.

Tip

Valuable items belong neither on deck nor in the saloon, where a rascal could collect the loose items in seconds. They are better stored in the cabin cupboards, and one should furthermore lock the yacht and fold away the gangway when going off, so at least another pair of hands would be needed to get on board. Incidentally, the bad guys also know that the ship's keys like to be left in the bucket in the stern locker, so that every crew member can have easy access.

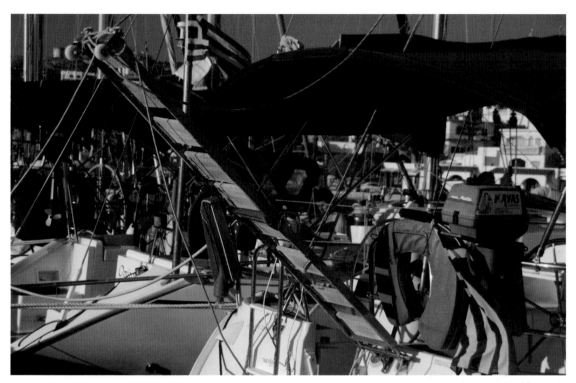

A hoisted gangway and a wallet that cannot be seen on one's person make things difficult for thieves.

In an anchorage it is easy to tell from afar which yacht still has crew on board and which do not. It's the one with the missing tender. But despite this, an anchor watchman might have been left behind, so the thieves have to be careful. If the on-board radio can be heard from afar, it could mean that someone is still on board, which could deter offenders from climbing on board.

Valuable jewelry should generally be left at home, since it seems to magically attract thieves. Cash can be carried in a money-belt. After use, store the tender back on board or at least winched half-way out of the water on a halyard.

Incidentally, in the Caribbean the boat boys guard the yacht quite effectively when the crew goes on land, in exchange for a small fee.

Conclusion: One can make things difficult for the thieves, but professionals can recognize a profitable yacht and empty it out in no time. Staying at home won't really help, since there will also be thieves doing their mischief. Thus, there is always a risk in every location.

Smoke-Free on Board as Well

Non-smoking skippers, and especially owners who are avid non-smokers, can tell you about it: smokers are on board. It isn't so bad in itself if the smoker sits far to the lee, blows the smoke away from the noses of the non-smokers and drops the ash into the water. But usually this is pure theory, since the ash always does what it wants and trickles onto the boat—despite all precautions. So, after a few days, small black mounds of cigarette ash end up in the tiniest corners, which are subsequently spread by feet throughout the entire yacht.

But even this is still not really that serious. Things only become serious when, together with the ash, hot embers fall onto the delicate gelcoat or even the teak deck, causing burn marks!

Not only does it result in ugly brown stains, which can't be polished out, it also burns the gelcoat, which consists of plastic after all, making it brittle and porous.

But to skippers, even users of snuff tobacco are a pain in the backside. With each snuff, only a part of the tobacco ends up in the nose. The rest puffs into the air and comes floating down onto the deck as fine dust. It then likes to collect in small depressions where it swells up through the help of some moisture. The resulting tobacco water etches itself into the gelcoat and forms unsightly and permanent speckles. The same can happen with fresh tobacco, so self-rollers should also take care if they don't want to end up in the skipper's bad books.

Good advice is to have some understanding when the yacht owner or skipper declares the yacht a smoke-free zone. It has—as we have just seen—nothing at all to do with a non-smokers being intolerant of smokers, but rather a well-founded danger that the yacht could be damaged. No owner should suffer burn-marks on his/her yacht. So go ashore when you want to roll, smoke, or snuff, because the ash or tobacco can still fall on the floor or deck at any time.

Small Gifts Preserve Friendship

Have you ever been abroad for a long period? Then you have probably noticed that on your return, you have an intense craving for home-cooked food.

Exotic foods in foreign countries may be all well and good, but nothing beats your favorite home-cooked meal. Similarly, the same happens to your countrymen working abroad: Tour guides, hotel and charter service center personnel, your skipper on board, and many others. They are all happy to receive a small culinary treat from home. It doesn't have to be a delicatessen from an exclusive shop—something small from the supermarket will do just fine.

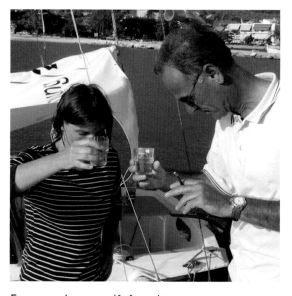

Everyone loves a gift from home.

Tip

There are three things that matter:

▶ The treat you bring should, of course, comply with the customs and regulations of the country you are traveling to.

This is mostly the case with preserves, cans, or other processed foods. Fresh items cannot be brought into the USA, for example, even if the fresh rolls taste very good. Even a Turkish customs official won't give you hassles over a can of pork.

▶ The item must be easy to carry. Securely contained goods also work the best in this respect.

▶ The food needs to have a long shelf life and not be susceptible to warmer temperatures (in the holiday destination).

Here is a small list of possible treats that won't stretch the holiday budget, but will ensure a great vacation with great friends, and possibly open some doors on the trip: Sturdy cheese, bread, mustard, smoked meats, preserved fish, pickles or other sweet-and-sour treats, or a bottle of good beer. This list can be further extended of course. But keep in mind that in many countries these foodstuffs can either not be found at all or are unbelievably expensive as imported goods. So, for example, a bottle of spiced pickles, which can be found for a few dollars at home, costs more than five dollars in Greece! Try to pack a small gift in your luggage and give it away as a present at some stage. You will see, the receiver will be overjoyed.

Everyone appreciates a souvenir.

About the Author

Hans Mühlbauer is an experienced long-distance
sailor and charter organizer. He can be contacted
at hans.muehlbauer@dmcreisen.de or 49-0821-
711124.

WWW.SCHIFFERBOOKS.COM

Nautical Etiquette & Customs 2nd Edition. Lindsay Lord. Here is a little book about nautical etiquette that will appeal to all those who sail for sport or pleasure, from the neophyte to the veteran boater. With a light but sure touch, marked by gentle humor, Lindsay Lord explores both the past and present state of yachting culture. He succeeds in extracting from the elaborate and sometimes extravagant mores of bygone years those practices that are sound and worth preserving. There are also apt descriptions of the protocol for the yacht club ashore, including such topics as launching parties, club commissioning, and even tipping.

Size: 5 1/2" x 8 1/2"	16 illustrations	128pp.
ISBN: 978-0-87033-356-9	Soft Cover	$8.95

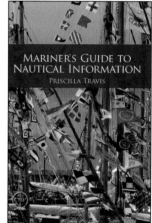

Mariner's Guide to Nautical Information Priscilla Travis. This alphabetically arranged reference work puts over 2,000 modern nautical topics and terms at your fingertips, with enough explanatory advice to be truly useful. Topics ranging from the Navigation Rules, cruising under sail and power, electronics, and communication, to safety, weather, technical topics, and commonly-used spoken nautical language make this book a comprehensive resource. The Topic Index helps you test your knowledge and learn more about a subject, and the extensive annotated bibliography identifies hundreds of relevant publications and Internet resources. These terms are illustrated with 173 color photographs and 11 line drawings. If you are thinking about getting started on the water, this book is for you. If you are already out there and dreaming about distant horizons, there is a wealth of information to help you become more competent, confident, and comfortable afloat. International emphasis is also incorporated for readers in Canada and across the pond.

Size: 6 x 9	190 color & 9 b/w photos	544pp.
ISBN: 978-0-87033-625-6	Hard Cover	$35

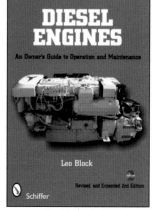

Diesel Engines: An Owner's Guide to Operations and Maintenance Revised and Expanded 2nd Edition. Leo Block. This practical book presents fundamental principles and identifies the separate systems (fuel, cooling, etc.). In this revision, urgent information is supplied for electronic diesel engines. It explores three fuel systems: low pressure, mechanical, and electronic. Checklists of required maintenance tasks are included, with explanations of engine operation: warm-up, normal running, and shutdown. This guide provides illustrations and step-by-step instructions. The explanation of the basic engine systems and routine tasks presented in *Diesel Engines*, augmented by the manufacturer's operating manual, puts the actual accomplishment of these jobs well within the capability of even a nontechnical boat owner. Special knowledge and tools are not required.

Size: 6 x 9	85 illustrations	160pp.
ISBN: 978-0-7643-3705-5	Soft Cover	$19.99

Sailing Fascination Heinrich Hecht. Text by Hans-Harald Schack. America's Cup races, regattas around the world, and Olympic sailing competitions are the classic yachting events where the most picturesque sailing takes place. This broad spectrum of yachting fascinates versatile professional photographer Heinrich Hecht. Over twenty years (1984–2008) of Hecht's work is presented here. Twelve chapters are organized specifically to show highlights of the sport: the sail, speed, classic beauty, dinghies and keelboats, the crew, regattas, sailors, the wind, waves, and light. These are themes illustrated by over 300 dynamic color photographs. Be transported through these brilliant images to far-flung races featuring extremely skillful, famous sailors.
Size: 11 3/4" x 9"   300+ color images   264pp.
ISBN: 978-0-7643-4268-4   Hard Cover $50.00

Lights, Shapes, & Signals for the Merchant Mariner: A Flash Card Study Guide Captain D. Green. Created to be small and compact for easy traveling, this study guide provides all the lights, shapes, and symbols used out in the sea. How do you signal that a vessel is in distress or has run aground? International signals and symbols are also provided, as is an alphabetical listing of phonetic and Morse Code. In addition to preparing marine students, this book is a valuable tool for the seasoned mariner or private boater who wants to sharpen their skills and make themselves safer and more prudent on the water. Its cargo-pocket size and lightly laminated pages means it can be taken on the "road" with the marine and endure in a maritime environment.
Size: 7 3/4" x 6"   302 color photos   560pp.
ISBN: 978-0-87033-628-7   Spiral Bound $34.99

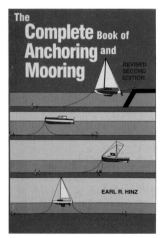

The Complete Book of Anchoring and Mooring Revised 2nd Edition Earl R. Hinz. The Complete Book of Anchoring and Mooring addresses anchoring systems, techniques, and permanent moorings for boats from twelve feet to eighty feet in length. It covers monohulls, multihulls, light displacement sailboats, cruisers, sportfishers, passagemakers, and workboats. In short, it is for all recreational and working boats in this size range. Since the last printing of this book, a number of revolutionary anchor concepts have appeared on the boating scene. These unique designs have shown exceptional performance when compared by a renowned testing agency with their contemporaries. Changes made to this revised second edition ensure its continued role as the state-of-the-art source book for the boating world.
Size: 6" x 9"   106 illustrations, 88 b/w photos, tables, and charts
index   352pp.
ISBN: 978-0-87033-539-6   Soft Cover $26.95

SCHIFFER PUBLISHING, LTD. 4880 LOWER VALLEY RD., ATGLEN, PA 19310 PHONE (610) 593-1777 FAX (610) 593-2002 E-MAIL: INFO@SCHIFFERBOOKS.COM

SCHIFFER BOOKS MAY BE ORDERED FROM YOUR LOCAL BOOKSTORE, OR THEY MAY BE ORDERED DIRECTLY FROM THE PUBLISHER.

PLEASE VISIT OUR WEB SITE CATALOG AT
WWW.SCHIFFERBOOKS.COM
OR WRITE FOR A FREE CATALOG.

Printed in China